Violence against Women

an annotated bibliography

A
Reference
Publication
in
Women's
Studies

Barbara Haber
Editor

Violence against Women

an annotated bibliography

CAROLYN F. WILSON

G.K.HALL &CO.

70 LINCOLN STREET, BOSTON, MASS.

Library of Congress Cataloging in Publication Data

Wilson, Carolyn F.
  Violence against women.

  Includes indexes.
  1. Women—United States—Crimes against—Abstracts.
2. Violence (Law)—United States—Abstracts. 3. Rape—
United States—Abstracts. 4. Wife abuse—United States
—Abstracts. 5. Incest—United States—Abstracts.
6. Pornography—United States—Abstracts. I. Title.
HV6250.4.W65W54   016.3628′3   81-6232
ISBN 0-8161-8497-6   AACR2

This publication is printed on permanent/durable acid-free paper
MANUFACTURED IN THE UNITED STATES OF AMERICA

Contents

Contents

The Author

Carolyn F. Wilson is a graduate of Smith College, has a Masters of Library Science degree from Pratt Institute, and has undertaken additional study at the University of Wisconsin Library School. As a staff member of Women's Education Resources, University of Wisconsin Extension, her interest has been in women-related issues. Her series of twelve packets on women's issues, published by the department, are distributed nationally to libraries and women's groups. With the packets as a focus, Ms. Wilson organized and coordinated a series of workshops for Wisconsin public and university librarians on methods and materials useful in responding to clients' questions on women-related issues. This project received the National University Extension Association's 1978 award for creative women's programming.

Preface

In the preface to the original 1978 pamphlet of the same title on which this book is based, Dr. Kathryn Clarenbach noted, "What is evident in the matter of rape and battering, on which the study concentrates, may be extended to all other forms of violence. Basically, violence, whatever its outward form, has its roots in the inequality between men and women." That statement holds for the present publication, which now includes, in addition to the subjects of battered women and rape, those of incest and pornography. Surely that message, stated or not, is inherent in all of the present material: Violence against women is rooted in inequality.

As in the original pamphlet, I have retrieved from several data bases hundreds of references to articles on violence against women (and children, in the case of incest) written from the perspectives of researchers in academic fields and in agency and other institutional settings, all of them dealing with abuse in its manifold forms. Besides computer printouts I have used other specialized tools to become familiar with a wide variety of subject matter. These aids include Women's Studies Abstracts, Current Contents, and the more general Social Science Index. Because this bibliography is directed to students in women's studies courses, I have emphasized journal literature likely to be found in most college and university libraries. Interlibrary loan makes those journals not in collections readily accessible. I have not, however, rejected popular literature sources. Regular routine searches have also been made of the Readers Guide to Periodical Literature and Public Affairs Information Service, for we must remember that some of the keenest observations on violence against women come from feminist writers whose work appears in popular magazines such as Ms.

The vast outpouring of scholarly and popular literature presents the bibliographer with a formidable task in keeping up to date with the material as well as making a judicious selection. What finally appear in this bibliography are my choices of current, representative articles and books, the most recent I could find, preferably those appearing between 1975 and August 1980. Yet a few new classics from the early seventies that opened people's eyes to the extent of sexual

Preface

abuse, such as Susan Brownmiller's <u>Against Our Will</u> and Susan Griffin's "Rape: The All-American Crime" have not been omitted.

A more basic reason for generally preferring studies from 1975 and later is that fewer chauvinistic overtones characterize these studies. By 1975 feminist thought had had a chance to filter through to the medical, police, and judicial systems where the most unrelievedly patriarchal beliefs held sway. The undeniable authenticity of feminist insights had made some few inroads even there, and the results are evident in later studies coming from those quarters. It should be noted that feminist research into the connection between pornography and violence against women began fairly recently, so that there are far fewer references to research in that area than there will be in the coming year(s).

Within the large subject categories, titles are grouped, as much as possible, according to their discussion from the point of view of the social sciences (sociology, psychology, social work), of the police and judiciary, and of the medical world. Most of these studies support to some degree the point of view of the Women's Movement. The divisions are admittedly not always clear-cut and there may be some overlap.

Two indexes, author/title and subject, follow the bibliographical listing. Numerals refer in all cases to the entry number rather than to the page number. A list of journals from which articles have been drawn may be found before the listing. Addresses are given for a few newsletter titles cited. It was my thought that because these newsletters are directed to a special audience, they may not yet be readily accessible.

Thanks to the University of Wisconsin-Extension for permission to use material that originally appeared in the 1979 pamphlet, <u>Violence against Women: Causes and Prevention. A Literature Search and Annotated Bibliography</u>, as a basis for the present book. A grant from the Wisconsin Council on Criminal Justice to Dr. Kathryn F. Clarenbach, Chair of Women's Educational Resources, University of Wisconsin-Extension, funded the publication of that pamphlet. My appreciation to the staff of Women's Education Resources for cheerful assistance at every stage.

My especial thanks and gratitude to Kay Clarenbach, whose wit and wisdom continue to smooth the way.

Journals Consulted

Aegis
Aggressive Behavior
American Ethnologist
American Journal of Diseases of Children
American Journal of Orthopsychiatry
American Journal of Psychiatry
American Journal of Psychoanalysis, The
American Journal of Psychotherapy
American Sociological Review
Archives of General Psychiatry
Archives of Sexual Behavior
Australian and New Zealand Journal of Psychiatry

Bulletin of the American Academy of Psychiatry and the Law

Child Welfare
Counseling Psychologist
Crime and Social Justice: Journal of Radical Criminology
Current

Dimensions in Health Service

Family Coordinator, The

Human Nature

Info Digest
Innovations
Intellect
International Journal of Health Services
International Social Science Journal

Journal of American Academy of Child Psychiatry
Journal of Applied Social Psychology
Journal of Clinical Psychiatry
Journal of College Student Personnel
Journal of Community Psychology

Journal of Consulting and Clinical Psychology
Journal of Family Law
Journal of Humanistic Psychology
Journal of Marriage and Family Counseling
Journal of Marriage and the Family
Journal of Personality
Journal of Personality and Social Psychology
Journal of Psychiatric Nursing and Mental Health
Journal of Sex Research, The
Journal of Social Issues
Journal of the History of Ideas

Medical Aspects of Human Sexuality
Medico-Legal Journal
Mother Jones
Ms. Magazine

New York State Journal of Medicine
Newspage

off our backs

Personality and Social Psychology Bulletin
Practitioner, The
Psychiatric Annals
Psychiatry
Psychology Today

Quarterly Journal of Speech

Ramparts
Resident and Staff Physician
Response

SANEnews
Science for the People
Science and Psychoanalysis
Second Wave, The: A Magazine of the New Feminism
Signs
Social Action and the Law
Social Casework
Social Problems
Social Science Information
Social Work
Social Work Today
Sociology and Social Research

Trial

University of Illinois Law Forum
USA Today

Journals Consulted

Victimology: An International Journal

Women and Health: The Journal of Women's Health Care
Women's Rights Law Reporter
Women's Work

Chapter 1
Introduction

This annotated bibliography enlarges upon a pamphlet of the same title, which appeared in 1978. By that time, the rape and battering of women had been recognized as severe forms of brutality and had become subjects for public discussion and media treatment as well as issues for activism by the Women's Movement. The consequences were some reform and many new research projects, some simple and some multilevel. Until that time, violence against women had seldom been discussed openly; however, with the raising of women's consciousness, the topic burst into the limelight of public scrutiny. Research into the causes of violence in general was not without precedent. Two Presidential Commissions had issued reports: in 1969 on the causes and prevention of violence in the United States, "To Establish Justice and Insure Domestic Tranquility"; and in 1970 on obscenity and pornography. Both reports had initially aroused heated discussion and controversy, but had ultimately faded into obscurity. Few people, men or women, had considered research into the causes of violence against women as sufficiently important in our patriarchal society to warrant the attention of public policymakers.

The Project on the Status and Education of Women of the Association of American Colleges sponsored the publication in 1975 of "A Survey of Research Concerns on Women's Issues" by Arlene Kaplan Daniels. An examination of this work discloses that not a single study of more than 300 listed in her bibliography mentioned either rape or battered women in its title. Nor did the publication's most pertinent sections, on marital status and the family or on health and life cycle issues, mention either subject as a possible area of concern.

Despite the omission in Daniels's monograph, 1975 was also the year of publication of _Against Our Will_ by Susan Brownmiller. Brownmiller perhaps best typifies contemporary feminist thinking. She has been attacked by some sociologists, who find in her views gaps and false assertions; yet she has continued to be strongly supported by others. Brownmiller has observed: "From prehistoric times to the present . . . rape has played a critical function. It is nothing more or less than a conscious process of intimidation by which all men keep all women in a state of fear" (entry 32), p. 15.

1

Introduction

The consciousness-raising techniques of the Women's Movement, if any single impulse may be singled out, were responsible for the sudden designation of violence against women as a major issue. One began to investigate the tradition of violence at home and on the street against all women. Consciousness-raising demonstrated over and over again how and why men dominate as well as how and why women accept their own inferior position.

The 1970s was the decade of the resurgence of feminism, with its strong support of equal rights legislation. These years witnessed the emergence of feminist activism in all arenas, of feminist scholarship in academia, and of increased research into the patriarchal system and its methods of social control over women. The study of the history of women cannot help but also reveal the history of patriarchy. The manifestations of patriarchy throughout the social fabric constituted important areas of interest to researchers and to students endeavoring to combat economic, educational, and political discrimination at one end of the continuum and increasing physical and psychological violence at the other.

Feminists were not alone in undertaking research into these subjects. Nevertheless, this bibliography purports to show that the results of feminist study, based upon intimate knowledge of discrimination and abuse unknown to men, form the criteria against which all other research on violence, a wide spectrum of studies in every discipline, must be judged for authenticity. The behavioral sciences (anthropology, psychology, sociology, and social work), criminal justice (police and the courts), and medicine (general, gynecology, and psychiatry) began to examine violence against women in new ways. Jennifer Fleming has noted that it is "relatively easy to use research instruments--scales, questionnaires, and personality inventories-- that have been utilized in earlier studies previously 'tested' for validity and reliability." Yet she also warns that the fact "that there is an underlying sexist bias inherent in their construction is frequently overlooked, and these instruments have been administered to battered women in some cases without question by traditionalist investigators" (entry 53), p. 344.

The original pamphlet from which this bibliography has grown nevertheless did not cover two other forms of abusive treatment of women: incest, or the sexual abuse principally of girl children; and pornography, or a graphic, sexually explicit kind of male entertainment, which serves primarily to suggest the brutalization of women. Within the last few years, both manifestations have become prominent subjects of public debate. Each of these topics merits its own section.

This bibliography concentrates on the period between 1975 and 1980. There are a few entries prior to 1975. In general, the more recent publications are emphasized, for as soon as the subject of violence against women became a public issue, a great many monographs and journal articles appeared. Many of the publications, especially those in book form, achieved sufficient prominence for the titles to reappear in many bibliographies. In the present bibliography, a decision has been made to avoid repeating others as much as possible.

This general, introductory, and highly selective section offers a number of diverse approaches to the subject of violence. Theoretical and empirical studies have been listed to illustrate the range and intensity of work that has been done in this field over the past five years.

Introduction

ANTHOLOGIES (SEVERAL DISCIPLINES)

1   CHAPMAN, JANE ROBERTS, and GATES, MARGARET, eds. The Victimi-
    zation of Women. Sage Yearbooks in Women's Policy Studies,
    vol. 3. Beverly Hills, Calif.: Sage Publications, 1978.
    282 pp. Bibliogs.
        Eleven essays by specialists on abusive behavior toward
    women and children and the overall effects of sexism upon
    the economy and upon the quality of life. Graphically
    demonstrates the need to change society. Offers a number
    of suggestions and possible solutions toward eliminating
    the worst manifestations of sexism in our society.

2   SADOFF, ROBERT L., ed. Violence and Responsibility: The
    Individual, the Family and Society. New York: SP Medical
    and Scientific Books, 1978, 139 pp.
        A collection of papers presented in 1976 at two separate,
    multidisciplinary conferences on "Violence in Families"
    and "Violence and Responsibility." Includes neurological-
    medical aspects of violence, psychodynamic factors, and
    sociolegal aspects of family violence.

3   SMART, CAROL, and SMART, BARRY, eds. Women, Sexuality, and
    Social Control. London and Boston: Routledge & Kegan
    Paul, 1978, 121 pp. Bibliog.
        An anthology of eight articles, which describe, from a
    variety of disciplines (including law and sociology), the
    low regard in which women have been held since early times.
    Beginning in the Middle Ages, for example, women who had
    formerly fulfilled a wide range of functions (from growing
    food and raw materials for production of household items to
    military defense of their homes) gradually had their roles
    reduced to dependency on their husbands. Especially note-
    worthy is the essay by Albie Sachs, "The Myth of Male Pro-
    tectiveness and the Legal Subordination of Women: An
    Historical Analysis."

4   VIANO, EMILIO C. Victims and Society. Washington, D.C.:
    Visage Press, 1976, 642 pp. Bibliog.
        Many chapters in this work were originally prepared for
    presentation at the International Study Institute on Victim-
    ology at Bellagio, Italy, in 1975. Each of the five parts
    is preceded by an overview of the area: Conceptual Issues,
    Research Methodology and Findings, The Victim and the Jus-
    tice System, Treatment and Prevention, Institutional Victim-
    ization. The forty-six chapters are oriented either around
    facts (empirical investigations, methodologies, analyses of
    concepts) or practice (policy recommendations, descriptive
    and evaluative reports of treatment and law). Victimology,
    a branch of criminology, presupposes the active role of the

victim in the crime. Such phrases as <u>victim precipitation</u>
and <u>victim provocation</u>, inherently derogatory terms, have
been replaced by such neutral terms as <u>victim participation</u>
and victim vulnerability to approximate more accurately
actual victim behavior.

CRIMINAL JUSTICE SYSTEM: ATTITUDES

5   DeCROW, KAREN. <u>Sexist Justice</u>. New York: Vintage Books,
        1974, 363 pp.
            A review of the many facets of American law that operate
        to the detriment of American women. Unfortunately, there
        is no index. Chapter notes and the text cite important
        cases and instances of the effect of patriarchal justice
        upon more than half of the population. Discusses rape and
        prostitution at length.

6   SADOFF, ROBERT L. "Violence in Families: An Overview."
        <u>Bulletin of the American Academy of Psychiatry and the Law</u>,
        4, no. 4 (1976):292-96.
            This paper introduces the several points of view ex-
        pounded in a 1976 symposium on "Medical, Legal and Psycho-
        social Aspects of Violence in Families." Presents arguments
        for the rehabilitation of the violent criminal as a worth-
        while effort--in contrast to studies that view such efforts
        as useless and wasteful of taxpayers' money: "The violent
        individual in families has to be dealt with by a number of
        medical, legal and social practitioners, including general
        physicians, psychiatrists, psychologists, sociologists,
        neurologists, lawyers and judges."

GENERAL ANTHROPOLOGICAL AND HISTORICAL STUDIES

7   BOULDING, ELISE. <u>The Underside of History: A View of Women
        Through Time</u>. Boulder, Colo.: Westview Press, 1976,
        829 pp. Bibliog.
            This 800-page encyclopedic book describes the lives and
        thoughts of many women who have overcome sexist barriers to
        make significant contributions, through all ages, from pre-
        historic times to the 1970s. Tables, illustrations, end-
        of-chapter notes, and selective bibliographies identify
        gratifyingly rich resources.

General Studies

8   DALY, MARY. <u>GYN/ECOLOGY: The Metaethics of Radical Feminism</u>.
    Boston: Beacon Press, 1978, 485 pp.
        This work by America's leading feminist philosopher-
    theologian severely criticizes and rejects patriarchal
    society and its institutions. At the same time, it cele-
    brates the creativity and potentiality of women and calls
    upon them to sever the bonds that result in their subjuga-
    tion. The style becomes very intense through its accumula-
    tion of examples of male oppressiveness.

9   FIGES, EVA. <u>Patriarchal Attitudes: The Case for Women in
    Revolt</u>. New York: Fawcett, 1970, 191 pp. Bibliog.
        An exposé of patriarchal myths and legends, from the
    Judaic tradition, beginning with the story of Adam's first
    wife, Lilith. Figes also includes Freud's theories of
    women's submissiveness. Identifies the sexual taboos of
    various cultures and fears of the insatiable, dominating
    woman that culminate in an all-powerful patriarchal society.
    Also describes the transformation of woman's role in the
    economic chain from being coequal with her husband in the
    home-craft system to a dependent after the Industrial Revo-
    lution. Shows how renowned theorists, such as Rousseau and
    Darwin, denigrate women to the advantage of men.

10 HARRIS, MARVIN. "Why Men Dominate Women." <u>The New York Times
    Magazine Section</u>, 13 November 1977, p. 46.
        Columbia University anthropologist Harris traces men's
    domination of women back to band and village societies.
    The domination did not occur because it is natural for men
    to be aggressive and take control. Domination is not bio-
    logically imperative nor genetically programmed. Nor is it
    an arbitrary social convention or a conspiracy to degrade
    women. Links warfare and male sexism to social inventions
    that functioned among primitive groups to prevent over-
    population and destruction of natural resources.

11 HAYS, H. R. <u>The Dangerous Sex: The Myth of Feminine Evil</u>.
    New York: G. P. Putnam's Sons, 1964, 397 pp. Bibliog.
        Background on the origin of the belief in women as
    property, rationalized by the story of the Fall, with
    Eve's deceit proving the falsity of women. Role of self-
    interest through the medieval marriage system whereby
    women became chattel. Unusual bibliography.

12 HIPPLER, ARTHUR E. "The North Alaska Eskimos: A Culture and
    Personality Perspective." <u>American Ethnologist</u> 1, no. 3
    (August 1974):449-69.

Socialization of Eskimo children tended to produce personalities that were at once dependent and cooperative, egocentric and violent. A principal concern in Eskimo life was the control of aggression. An indulgent early childrearing was succeeded by a second period of harsh teasing by relatives and even the mother. Such treatment led to frustration and rage, which was then controlled by a smiling demeanor. The child was impressed with the dual nature of the universe, viewed as nurturant yet occasionally unpredictable. Eskimo men treated women quite cruelly at times and nearly always as inferiors; Hippler sees this as the expression of repressed rage against an inconsistent mother.

13 LAING, R. D. <u>The Politics of the Family and Other Essays</u>. New York: Vintage Books, 1969, 133 pp. Bibliog.
    Background book. Theorizes that families receive instructions on behavior across generations, through a "secret" communications network "dissociated from the official verbal communiques."

14 LESSE, STANLEY. "The Status of Violence Against Women: Past, Present and Future Factors." <u>American Journal of Psychotherapy</u> 32, no. 2 (April 1979):190-200.
    Comprehensive review of the relationships between men and women, from the hunting phase of society, through the agricultural and industrial eras, into present-day automation and cybernation. Treats related biological, social, economic, and technical changes. Suggests the current, increasing violence against women will subside in the twenty-first century. The next century's postindustrial technology will so absorb men and women into the production of goods and services that male-female power conflict will fade as an issue.

15 PADDOCK, JOHN. "Studies on Antiviolent and 'Normal' Communities." <u>Aggressive Behavior</u> 1 (1975):217-33.
    Limited preliminary studies have identified several communities in the valley of Oaxaca, Mexico that successfully control interpersonal violence without the formal police and judicial apparatus customary in industrial societies, even though surrounded by towns exhibiting a "normal" level of violence. Unique to the antiviolent communities are lack of machismo, more relaxed practices of childrearing, a much stronger social role for women, and opposition to outside influences within the community (such as the government's building of new secondary schools).

Introduction

General Studies

16   RICH, ADRIENNE. On Lies, Secrets, and Silence. Selected
      Prose 1966-1978. New York: W. W. Norton, 1979, 310 pp.
           All of these essays contain many examples of conscious
      and unconscious misogyny and of the various ways women have
      attempted, not often very successfully, to deal with sym-
      bolic and real assaults upon their minds and bodies. Like
      Daly, Rich has broken the silence on important topics.

17   THOMAS, KEITH. "The Double Standard." Journal of the History
      of Ideas 20, no. 2 (April 1959):195-216.
           This article expounds the notion of women as property in
      eighteenth-century England. The double standard operated
      to the advantage of men not only through prostitution but
      also through divorce and the inheritance of land. Uses
      primary and secondary sources to show how men maintained
      their sexual freedom while single women remained virgin and
      married women faithful to their husbands.

18   WIN NEWS: WOMEN'S INTERNATIONAL NETWORK. Lexington, Mass.:
      Fran P. Hosken, Editor.
           An open, participatory network by, for, and about women,
      WIN NEWS was begun in 1975 during the International Women's
      Year (IWY) Conference in Mexico City and contains reports
      from over 100 countries and the IWY Congress held in East
      Berlin that October. Carries ongoing columns, including
      one on women and violence. Along with Diana Russell,
      Hosken initiated discussion of genital mutilation (clito-
      ridectomy). For subscriptions, write to Fran P. Hosken,
      187 Grant Street, Lexington, Mass. 02173.

LEGISLATIVE CONCERNS

19   NATIONAL COMMISSION ON THE OBSERVANCE OF INTERNATIONAL WOMEN'S
      YEAR. The Spirit of Houston; The First National Women's
      Conference: An Official Report to the President, the
      Congress and the People of the United States. Washington,
      D.C.: U.S. Government Printing Office, 1978, 391 pp.
      Bibliog.
           This report contains the National Plan of Action, whose
      twenty-six-plank program includes substantial sections on
      violence toward women in terms of battering and rape. In
      a concentrated way, the planks cover the historical treat-
      ment of these crimes, current legislative concerns, sugges-
      tions for emergency help, and legislative measures for
      eradicating these elements of a sexist society.

20 Response. Washington, D.C.: Center for Women Policy Studies.
    Monthly newsletter to inform groups concerned with
    domestic violence and sexual assault about current liter-
    ature, funding sources, ongoing research, conferences, and,
    most important, innovative and effective programs and tech-
    niques. Address: CWPS, 2000 P St. N.W., Suite 508,
    Washington, D.C. 20036.

21 SANEnews (Spouse Abuse North East News). Middletown, Conn.:
    Domestic Violence Component of the Community Health Center,
    Inc.
    A newsletter to inform groups concerned with domestic
    violence and sexual assault in much the same way as Response,
    the organ of the Center for Women Policy Studies, does. Re-
    views domestic legislation, funding sources, and regional
    news of the subject. Provides personal profiles of people
    who are active in reform. Address: Community Health
    Center, Box 1076, Middletown, Conn. 06457.

PSYCHOLOGICAL STUDIES

22 FROMM, ERICH. The Anatomy of Human Destructiveness. New York:
    Holt, Rinehart & Winston, 1973, 526 pp. Bibliog.
    This traditional study treats the problem of aggression.
    Distinguishes defensive, "benign" aggression for survival
    of the individual and the species from malignant aggression
    for destruction and cruelty, the latter shown only by
    humans. Adheres to a sociobiological point of view. Uses
    a revised psychoanalytic method and avoids the "instinc-
    tivistic" concepts of Freud's theory. Studies various
    forms of character-rooted, malignant aggression through
    the examples of Stalin, Himmler, and Hitler.

23 GELLES, RICHARD J. "Methods for Studying Sensitive Family
    Topics." American Journal of Orthopsychiatry 48, no. 3
    (July 1978):408-24.
    A discussion of the difficulties in obtaining reliable
    data on violence in the family. Discusses each method
    practiced today and outlines limits of each approach. Some
    of the obstacles include the following: private nature of
    family and the difficulty of locating subjects and engaging
    family cooperation. Proposes methods for pursuing research
    on taboo subjects. Warns of risks in the study of sensitive
    topics in order to find creative, humane solutions to eth-
    ical problems.

Psychological Studies

24   HAVENS, LESTON L. "Youth, Violence, and the Nature of Family
     Life." <u>Psychiatric Annals</u> 2, no. 2 (February 1972):18-29.
        Historical, biological, genetic survey of the way a
     pattern of violence is revealed over generations of fami-
     lies. Suggests that it seems to be relayed through body
     type, temperament, and perhaps special inherited features.
     Psychical and social mechanisms and psychological trans-
     mission also play a part. Acknowledges that nothing has
     been verified.

25   MILLER, JEAN BAKER. <u>Toward a New Psychology of Women</u>. Boston,
     Mass.: Beacon Press, 1976, 143 pp.
        This book enables women to perceive themselves anew and
     to recognize in themselves values that have been underrated
     thus far. Defines creativity and power in a new way. Adop-
     tion of the attitudes defined by Baker would halt violence
     against women. Background for new thinking about women's
     roles.

26   ROSENBLUH, EDWARD S. "Crisis Techniques for Everyone."
     <u>Innovations</u> 3, no. 2 (1976):38.
        Describes common methods of dealing with violence devel-
     oped by a Louisville chapter of the National Conference of
     Christians and Jews and university mental health depart-
     ments with lecturers from various disciplines. Presents
     techniques of role playing and sociodrama among other
     methods. Applicable to all institutions, could be used
     by prison guards and nurses.

27   SAUL, LEON J. "Personal and Social Psychopathology and the
     Primary Prevention of Violence." <u>American Journal of
     Psychiatry</u> 128, no. 12 (June 1972):1578-81.
        A strongly patriarchal view by a Freudian psychoanalyst.
     Emphasizes that children reared with love and respect mature
     adequately into loving, responsible, and productive spouses,
     parents, and citizens. Adults who cause violence in the
     world have not been so nurtured. Yet advocates no changes
     in the present social system.

28   SHAINESS, NATALIE. "Vulnerability to Violence: Masochism as
     a Process." <u>American Journal of Psychotherapy</u> 33, no. 2
     (April 1979):174-89.
        Notes that the type of violence in the home that has
     elicited the interest of women's groups often indicates
     that the offender is striking out against an incorporated,
     hated, mother-image. Freud had elaborated the concept of
     feminine masochism as a universal trait of women, who seek
     or enjoy punishment. "His concept has been re-examined and

Introduction

Sociological Perspectives

translated into a more or less universal, culturally determined process women use in dealing with certain situations,
suggesting that their gender restriction in society has
played a part in the evolution of a submissive and self-
destructive style which does indeed increase their vulnerability to violence. This tendency can be observed in many
everyday interchanges, in which the fear of men--particularly
as authority figures--leads to difficulty."

SOCIOLOGICAL PERSPECTIVES

29 ARCHER, DANE, and GARTNER, ROSEMARY. "Violent Acts and
Violent Times: A Comparative Approach to Postwar Homicide
Rates." American Sociological Review 41 (December 1946):
937-63.
Many researchers have considered the possibility that
waging war could heighten domestic violence and postwar
homicide in combatant societies.

30 BARKAS, J. L. Victims. New York: Scribners, 1978, 250 pp.
Bibliog.
Barkas became a victimologist after the brutal murder of
her brother by a mugger who was never apprehended. Pas-
sionate thoughtful study of the devastating impact upon
victims, their families, and their friends of the outrageous
treatment they receive from the present criminal justice
system. Elaborates the "just world" hypothesis. The "get-
what-they-deserve" attitude of many police departments makes
the victim the scapegoat. The frequently misguided rehabil-
itation efforts are often wasted upon the offender. Wide-
ranging bibliography of material on treatment of criminal
and victim from earliest times.

31 BOULDING, ELISE. "Women and Social Violence." International
Social Science Journal 30, no. 4 (1978):801-15.
The world will be more peaceful when women share combat
and policing roles with men, when economic opportunity is
equal for both, and when the law protects. But the arche-
typical patriarchal family has provided a societal model
for the myth of the conquering hero and the heroic rapist.
Women in such a society are thought to be protected property
or to present erotic opportunity. Either status reduces
women to objects and creates a set of social relations that
produce emotional infantilism in women and men. Assuming
the roles available in a violence-oriented society, women

11

Sociological Perspectives

will inevitably act as victims and men as aggressors. In
the short run, as a transition phenomenon, violent behavior
will increase among women, who will test new opportunities.
Boulding believes that the androgynous role model still
promises a more fully human growth.

32   BROWNMILLER, SUSAN. Against Our Will: Men, Women, and Rape.
      New York: Simon and Schuster, 1975, 472 pp. Bibliog.
          The impact of this book has been widespread. Written
      from a feminist perspective, it is a history of rape with
      special focus upon the United States. Describes male power
      over women: its evolution in the legal system; its use as
      a weapon of war and as a continuing means of social control.
      Already a classic of the new feminism.

33   THE COALITION TO STOP INSTITUTIONAL VIOLENCE. "The Worcester
      Ward: Violence Against Women." Science for the People,
      November/December 1978.
          The Coalition is a group of feminists in the Boston area
      who are engaged in advocacy for prisoners and psychiatric
      inmates. They successfully delayed the construction of a
      proposed behavior modification unit for women in a Worcester,
      Massachusetts mental institution. The proposed unit was
      described as a small, maximum security "treatment" facility
      for "violent" women. An instance of a thwarted attempt at
      social control by traditional psychiatry. Such control is
      described at length in Phyllis Chesler's Women and Madness
      (New York: Doubleday, 1972).

34   CORNING, PETER A., and CORNING, CONSTANCE HELLYER. "Toward a
      General Theory of Violent Aggression." Social Science
      Information 11, no. 3/4 (1972):7-35. Published under the
      auspices of International Social Science Council and
      UNESCO. The Hague, Netherlands: Mouton & Co.
          This scholarly study addresses far more than the causes
      of violence toward women. Describes genetic and biological-
      evolutionary factors that account for human violence, as
      well as sociological theories offered in explanation.
      Basic background reading.

35   COSER, LEWIS A. "Violence and the Social Structure." Science
      and Psychoanalysis 6:30-42. Violence and War With Clinical
      Studies. London and New York: Grune & Stratton, 1963,
      201 pp.
          Marginally relevant to question at hand. Contains some
      good points about violence in revolutions. Argues that in
      homicide, that is personal violence, women have internalized
      the assumption of their lower status. Where traditional

expectations have been shattered (as in revolutions),
women need no longer accept inferior status. Revolution
provides them with the occasion to assert their equality.

36 GOODE, W. J. "Force and Violence in the Family." <u>Journal of
Marriage and the Family</u> 33, no. 4 (November 1971):624-36.
   Nearly all of this issue is devoted to violence and the
family. Goode's introductory essay maintains that "violence is itself a resource which can be used to achieve
desired ends. It tends to be used when other resources
(such as money, respect, love, or shared goals) are lacking
or found to be insufficient." This philosophical-historical
study is useful in its comparing and contrasting of family
socialization in terms of desired ends during different
periods under various kinds of government.

37 OWENS, D. M., and STRAUS, M. A. "The Social Structure of
Violence in Childhood and Approval of Violence as an Adult."
<u>Aggressive Behavior</u> 1, no. 2 (1975):193-211.
   Based upon data from a national sample survey conducted
for the Commission on the Causes and Prevention of Violence.
Investigates the relationship between three aspects of exposure to violence in childhood (observing, being a victim,
and committing violence) with approval of violence as an
adult. The amount experienced in childhood is a contribut-
ing factor to the development and maintenance of cultural
norms that support the use of violence in face-to-face
situations.

Chapter 2
Battered Women

Everyone knows that the plight of battered women is not new. The issue of the abuse and subordination of women has been treated differently over time for various reasons. Justification for the maltreatment has been advanced through religious doctrine and civil codes. It has been based upon such grounds as the presence of evil spirits, woman's innate wickedness, the mysteriousness of women and the right of husbands and fathers to demand obedience and to mete out punishment.

J. J. Gayford, an English psychiatrist who has studied wife abuse extensively, includes in a long listing of references to marital violence the following: "In 1521, a Mr. Justice Brooke is quoted as stating that if a man beats an outlaw, a traitor, a pagan, a villain, or his wife, it is dispunishable" (entry 49), p. 122. Gayford provides evidence that upper-class women were also victims of violence. For example, Caroline Norton, an upper-class feminist writer of the mid-nineteenth century, was pushed downstairs while pregnant.

In The Subjection of Women (1869), John Stuart Mill decried the the conditions whereby a man could commit almost any atrocity against his wife without punishment, but she could not escape from her total dependency upon him. Much earlier, in folk culture, there were instances of wife battering, as exemplified in a sixteenth-century song by Orlando de Lassus, "The Troubles of Marriage," according to which, "when my husband gets home he beats me as though this were my fated vocation. He chases me through the street, and I fear he'll kill me."

In her introduction to The Victimation of Women (entry 1), p. 11, Attorney Margaret Gates, director of the Center for Women Policy Studies, clarifies the disparate power relationship whereby from earliest times women pledged obedience and fidelity to their male protectors who saved them from being carried off by the enemy for their value as breeders. Abuse begins when women do not meet the modern equivalents of obedience and fidelity. Even today some women oppose equality and desire continued dependence upon their husbands. Gates characterizes this as a reversion to the submissiveness that

15

our state of development no longer requires and that continues the socialization of women as inferiors, to their own and to society's detriment.

Katherine Saltzman, initiator and director of the Denver Coalition Against Sexual Assault, writes in The Victimization of Women: "Female victimization could be viewed as a problem with manageable boundaries, amenable to specific solutions if the perpetrators were aberrant and if the criminal justice process could be effectively employed." But, she continues, there is a "widespread network of attitudes and social codes that provide a firm foundation for the enactment of violence on women by men" (entry 1), p. 278.

Today, one of the greatest continuing obstacles to eliminating violence is the inconclusiveness of the statistics. Intelligent, effective programs of prevention and research into the causes must, they claim, be based upon facts that reveal the magnitude of the problem: where and when the violence occurs, the extent of repeated acts, and the circumstances preceding and during assaults on women. The National Women's Conference (1977), the U.S. Commission on Civil Rights (1978), and the reports of several Congressional Hearings have strongly recommended that such data be collected and disseminated. Women must feel safe and protected in reporting freely their victimization. Numerous studies have verified this as a basic reason why accurate data are not available. Realistic profiles of criminals and victims will be available for research only after the number of prosecutions is significant.

Reliable national estimates on the number of battered women vary from 4.7 to 15 million. Other estimates provided by the Law Enforcement Assistance Administration (LEAA)--including those by judges, attorneys, and domestic relations counselors--suggest that fifty percent of American wives are battered. It is now well known that cases occur at all levels of society, not exclusively among the working class, as assumed in the past. Statistics on rape are also inconclusive. It is believed that three to ten times as many occur as are reported.

Del Martin, a leading feminist authority on battered women, was among the first to publicize how far-reaching the abuse is. In her essay in The Victimization of Women (entry 1), Martin urges police to adopt a thorough recordkeeping system so that figures may be consistently tallied nationwide. It is important to separate wife-beating incidents from other categories of domestic disturbance. The relationship between victim and offender should be noted and tabulated under various categories, for example, whether it is that of spouse. Incidents should be cross-referenced by name and address. Thus, the police dispatcher can run a computerized check for previous reports involving the same parties and determine the degree of danger. Once on the scene, Martin continues, the investigating officer should carefully gather evidence and be aware of all possible corroborating witnesses. Under no circumstances should police assume, as they have done so frequently in the past, that the victim will drop the charges and therefore fail to make a full report. A detailed report filed in every instance will help establish a uniformity in statistics for future use and eliminate the unreliable figures that hamper people working in this area.

The dearth of adequate records on wife abuse is one of the fundamental problems of the criminal justice system. Yet some of the system's members are now learning in training sessions given by feminist task forces of the need for a complete picture of what happened, one that does not gloss over or play down the facts of intra-family violence. For the police are not exempt from the sex-role socialization that deems the man's role superior in virtually every respect to the woman's and believes that violence between men and women is not necessarily punishable.

Sex-Role Socialization as a Factor in Violence
    Influential researchers into aggression in animal behavior (Konrad Lorenz, Robert Ardrey, Desmond Morris) and human behavior (Freud and his school) assert that aggression is instinctual. In contrast, social psychologists and feminists--Brownmiller and others-- challenge the ethological and psychoanalytic view and claim that aggression resulting in violence is learned behavior. They maintain that sex-role socialization is the chief cause of male violence and female submission to it. Marvin E. Wolfgang offers this general definition of socialization: "Socialization . . . is the process of cultural transmission, of relaying through the social funnel of family and friends a set of beliefs, attitudes, values, speech and habits" (entry 92), p. 317.

In fact, present sex-role socialization is the most pervasive influence in Western society, strongest in its hold and most unyielding to change. Women's status has been referred to as "the final inequality." A clear example is resistance to the Equal Rights Amendment, a cornerstone for building improvements into our social system and eliminating sex-role stereotyping. Already debated for seven years, it is a principal target in a few states where the strong sex-role-socialization beliefs of its opponents cause legislators and voters to oppose equality for women and men and obstinately to reject its passage.

Social psychologist Murray A. Straus relates a well-known sexist joke: "One woman asked another why she felt her husband didn't love her anymore. Her answer: 'He hasn't bashed me in a fortnight.' At a higher literary level, plays provide many examples of the marriage license as a hitting license norm, including several by G. B. Shaw . . ." (entry 88), p. 57. He expands upon nine specific ways whereby the cultural norms and values of the Western world reinforce the right of the male to use violence and the inability of women to

escape from abusive situations. They are worth enumerating because
they largely reflect the opinions of most students on the subject:
(1) The defense of male authority. Men believe they are superior;
however, when this is demonstrated to be untrue, they resort to
physical violence, the "ultimate resource." (2) Compulsive masculinity. The desire to degrade and humiliate women often is the
motivating force, especially in rape. The mother's exclusive role
in child rearing causes a fundamental difficulty for males, who com-
pensate by becoming supermale. (3) Economic constraints and discrimination in employment. These allow some women little choice other
than to remain with an abusive husband and continue to endure physical
attacks. The alternative is poverty. (4) Burden of child care.
This may keep women out of the job market and thus dependent on an
abusive husband. (5) Myth of the single-parent household. This involves the belief that children are harmed if raised by only one
parent, and thus constrains abused women to remain in a marriage.
(6) Preeminence of role of wife for women. Only women who are married are respected within society. (7) Negative self-image. Women
fear achievement, which evokes feelings of guilt when they contemplate
out-of-home-pursuits. (8) Women as children. Although the concept
of women-as-property is no longer part of the legal system as it was
for so long, elements of this outlook linger; for example, women are
thought to need men to care for them. (9) Male orientation of the
criminal justice system. The socialization of the police and judiciary with the very characteristics described here virtually guarantees that few women will be able to secure legal relief.

Straus strongly advocates assertiveness training for women as an
important step in the direction of sexual equality and emphasizes the
need for men to perceive not only the advantages but also the "burdens
and restraints" of the traditional male role. Only then will there be
less violence in the world and in the family.

Straus finds (retroactive) support for his theories in the earlier
work of William J. Goode, sociologist at Columbia University (entry
36). Both Goode and Wolfgang maintain that all societies make clear
the acceptable limits to violence. Wolfgang writes further: "the
use of physical force by parents to restrain and punish children is
permissible, tolerated, and encouraged, and is thereby part of the
normative process by which every society regulates its child rearing."
He delineates the ultimate use of force in war and its connection to
force in civil life: "When the front-line instruments of war become
part of the physical features of a child's life space, when cannons,
rifles, grenades and soldiers are moved from real battlefields to
the mind of the child and the plastic world of his playroom and are
among the relatively few objects touched and manipulated by the child
in the process of becoming, then some set of values associated with
the legitimacy and recognition of the superiority of violent activity
is transmitted. What is not empirically clear is the extent to which
such transmission is later translated into violence by the child, as
a child, youth or adult. As a legislator, father, policeman or any

other role actor, he is still the carrier of attitudes related to
that play activity, unless contrary values have intervened" (emphasis
added). Wolfgang indicts women for inculcating these attitudes. In
encouraging boys to act like little men and not to cry when hurt,
mothers may be preparing them to be insensitive to being assaulted
or assaulting others as well as to endure adversity with strength.

Professional football and hockey also give evidence of our culture's acceptance of violence and brutality, for both the players and
the spectators display a bloodthirstiness reminiscent of the old
Roman arena. The emotional and highly successful opposition to gun
control legislation further indicates the tenacity of this acceptance.

Other Views of Violence in Personality Development

Bruce Rounsaville, Department of Psychiatry, Yale University
Medical School, contrasts his hypothesis of the cause of wife beating
with sociological theories of masculine/feminine role-socialization
(entry 69). While admitting that evidence also supports theories such
as Straus's, Rounsaville views family violence as a "final common
pathway of multiple determinants." While as individuals, the husband
may not be violent and the wife may be unwilling to tolerate abuse,
once enmeshed in a "dyadic relationship," and marriage is a most in-
tense relationship, a dynamic is created whereby violence occurs
regularly.

In most cases, women had been warned early in the marriage of
potential physical abuse. "The stable, enduring aspect of the battering relationship is remarked upon by all those who have studied it
and constitutes the most important feature to explain and aim interventions toward."

Some social caseworkers also recognize that patriarchal society
is riddled with attitudes of male dominance/female submissiveness.
But it has been difficult for this profession to shed its longstand-
ing belief that the home should be preserved and the family maintained
at whatever cost.

In upholding the home as the ideal social unit, social work and
the mental health professions have also been careful not to meddle
with minority group tradition, even in those instances when the tradition accepts wife abuse as a fact of life. But feminist theory is
making inroads into social casework and the mental health professions
as it has into the medical profession and the criminal justice system.
Many professionals now reject traditional attitudes and are receptive
to innovative treatment for both abusive husbands and victim wives.
Beverly Nichols recommends the hiring of more professionals from
ethnic minorities, who will understand whatever elements of the wife-
as-property notion may be present (entry 83). The special November
1976 issue of Social Work (entry 94) discusses battered women and
rape. Articles on both subjects address the need for consciousness-
raising of agency staffs and of advocacy for abused wives.

19

A <u>Directory of Programs Providing Services to Battered Women</u> is published by the Center for Women Policy Studies, a multifaceted project partially funded by the Law Enforcement Assistance Administration (LEAA). Estimates in late 1979 of shelters or refuges in the entire United States ranged from 200 to 300. Many of these are crowded and uncomfortable. The facilities are usually insufficient to meet the demand of women and their children who urgently need them. Despite their shortcomings, shelters are highly regarded and function as community resources. Unfortunately, money to keep them operating and to increase their numbers has been scarce. Del Martin claims that less than one-fifth of one percent of the billions of dollars granted by private foundations support women's projects such as this (entry 1), p. 120.

The types of women who seek shelter in these facilities is the subject of speculation and research. Certainly, it requires courage to leave a partner who provides financial support, however meager or generous. Many months of anguished evaluation may pass before a woman can decide whether or not to return home, whether or not to file charges, whether to continue or terminate the marriage. Capabilities to deal with these decisions vary. Observers agree, however, that battered women share one characteristic: they do not enjoy abuse. Barbara Star concludes her study on the personalities of battered women as follows: "Perhaps the findings holding the greatest significance for future research are those that offer an alternative to the masochism theory. The battered women in this study showed no signs of being submissive people, instead they scored within the normal range of the submissive-assertive continuum. They were, however, women who repressed anger, were timid, were emotionally reserved, and had low coping abilities. These factors point to passivity, rather than the need for maltreatment, as the more appropriate rationale underlying the endurance of physical abuse" (entry 71), p. 42.

Each annotation appears under a specific section heading. Yet it is perhaps misleading to attempt to categorize the entries in this way. Most of the studies are, in effect, interdisciplinary and do not fit neatly into psychological, sociological, legislative, or any other categories. Indeed, most frequently, the studies contain elements of several.

ANTHOLOGIES

38   GELLES, RICHARD J. Family Violence. Beverly Hills, Calif.:
        Sage Publications, 1979, 219 pp.
           This volume brings together ten previously unpublished
        essays (revised and updated) and one new essay on family
        violence. The essays are products of three closely-
        related research projects on why women stay, why preg-
        nant women are so often victims, and the incidence of
        marital rape. "The Truth About Husband Abuse" applies
        Steinmetz's controversial and severely criticized data,
        which showed that more husbands were beaten than wives
        (see entry 86), in an attempt to understand the real mean-
        ing of abuse. Employs a psychodynamic model to identify
        personality traits and character disorders. Notes that
        others have developed sociological, social psychological,
        ecological, and various multidimensional theories of vio-
        lence and abuse. In the 1970s, the most common model
        appears to have been a social psychological approach.

39   MARTIN, J. P., ed. Violence and the Family. New York:
        J. Wiley & Sons, 1978, 369 pp.
           This is a collection of primarily British studies on
        the difficulty of formulating policies about family vio-
        lence. Summarizes studies of child abuse. Recounts inter-
        views with battered women who have left home for refuges.
        Asserts that the need for refuges should take precedence
        over funding for research. Discusses reasons for family
        violence, from media influence to psychological factors.
        Goals of the collections are (1) to reveal what is known
        about family violence and to consider this knowledge from
        psychological and sociological perspectives; (2) to describe
        and discuss policies and practices that may help to prevent
        or mitigate the sufferings of the victims; and (3) to con-
        tribute to a longer-term process of education, both for
        professionals and the general public, regarding family
        violence.

40   MOORE, DONNA M., ed. Battered Women. Beverly Hills, Calif.:
        Sage Publications, 1979, 232 pp. Bibliog.
           This collection by experts--Del Martin, Leonore Walker,
        Eva Jefferson Paterson, Sandra Blair, Fran Pepitone-Rockwell,
        and the editor Donna Moore--unites in one text the complex
        web of legal, social policy, personal, and psychological
        perspectives. Students in many disciplines, including
        social work, pastoral and psychological counseling, nursing,
        and law enforcement will find the volume useful. The
        appendices include the handbook of Las Casas de las Madres
        (a California shelter) on the rights of battered women, an
        excellent annotated bibliography, and a summary of results

Anthologies

from a questionnaire concerning experiences with and attitudes about battering (taken by the participants of a conference on the subject).

41 ROY, MARIA, ed. Battered Women: A Psychosociological Study of Domestic Violence. New York: Van Nostrand Reinhold, 1977, 334 pp. Bibliog.
Anthology of articles written by members of many different professions dealing with wife abuse; collected by Maria Roy, the founder and director of a crisis center for battered women in New York City. Articles on the history of wife beating, demographic characteristics of battered women, a comparison of wife and husband beating, the neurology of explosive rage, legal concerns and solutions, and trends in prevention.

42 STEINMETZ, SUZANNE K., and STRAUS, MURRAY A., eds. Violence in the Family. New York: Dodd Mead and Co., 1974, 337 pp. Bibliog.
A selective collection of readings edited and introduced by two sociologists who have researched and written extensively on violence. Considers studies on violence between spouses and between other kin, and on the family as the training ground for societal violence. The general introduction, "Social Myth and Social System in the Study of Intrafamily Violence," examines a variety of theories on family organization that contribute to an understanding of violence.

BIBLIOGRAPHIES

43 ABRAHAMSON, CATHERINE. Spouse Abuse: An Annotated Bibliography. Washington, D.C.: Center for Women's Policy Studies, 1977, 20 pp.
This bibliography cites literature through 1976, considering a dozen widespread themes. Represents the views of sociologists, psychologists, feminists, police, lawyers, and crisis intervention personnel. Prefatory remarks identify a pressing need for intensive, additional research and valid statistics to enable people to formulate hypotheses and present practical solutions. Good examples of Abrahamson's recommendations are works by Jennifer Fleming (entry 53) and Leonore Walker (entry 75). Has both annotated and unannotated lists of books and reports on violence in general, both historical and background material.

44   HOWARD, PAMELA F. <u>Wife Beating: A Selected, Annotated Bib-</u>
         <u>liography</u>. San Diego, Calif.: Current Bibliography Series,
         1978, 57 pp.
         Although intended primarily for the lay person, would
      also be useful to organizations and researchers concerned
      with the problems of abused women. Rather unusual in list-
      ing newspaper articles not often found in bibliographies.
      Also includes a selected list of agencies that provide
      brochures, papers, packets, and other printed materials.
      Available through the publisher, Box 2709, San Diego,
      California 92112.

45   JOHNSON, CAROLYN; FERRY, JOHN; and KRAVITZ, MARJORIE, comps.
         <u>Spouse Abuse: A Selected Bibliography</u>. Rockville, Md.:
         National Criminal Justice Service, 1978, 61 pp.
         This comprehensive, free bibliography highlights the
      problem of spouse abuse and the various forms of inter-
      vention currently available. Presented in two parts:
      "The Nature of the Problem" annotates material describing
      family violence, analyzing causes and suggesting changes;
      "Intervention" annotates articles on the role of the justice
      system, the options available to victims, and the shelter
      models. A helpful feature is a list of publishers of both
      periodicals and books from whom copies of cited material
      may be obtained. All cited documents are in the collection
      of the National Criminal Justice Reference Service. Most
      are available to the interested person through either a
      free microfiche from NCJRS or interlibrary loan (Try the
      public, academic, or organization library). Also includes
      a list of resource agencies and organizations that are
      addressing the issue of spouse abuse. Contact National
      Criminal Justice Reference Service, Box 6000, Rockville,
      Md. 20850.

46   LYSTAD, MARY H. <u>Violence at Home. An Annotated Bibliography</u>.
         Rockville, Md.: National Institute of Mental Health, 1974,
         95 pp.
         Books and articles of a scientific nature on violence in
      the family, published, for the most part, between 1964 and
      1974. Includes studies of theoretical issues related to
      such violence; of the incidence of family violence; of
      violence between particular family members--husband and
      wife, parent and child, siblings; of violence and social
      structure, violence and socialization, and violence and
      social pathology; and on the need for and effectiveness of
      social services to discordant families offered by a wide
      variety of professional helpers from neighborhood police
      officer to emergency ward physician. A diversified group
      of studies whose current interest is reduced by the cutoff
      date.

Bibliographies

47 PETHICK, JANE. <u>Battered Wives: A Select Bibliography</u>.
   Toronto: University of Toronto, 1979, 114 pp.
   Deals with violence in the family from assault to murder;
   the social and legal aspects of the problem; studies and
   research on abusers and abused; police intervention in
   family crises; and solutions offered by various agencies
   or self-help groups in the community. Emphasizes scholarly
   literature in American, Australian, British, and Canadian
   publications of the 1970s. Includes some earlier materials
   and some from the popular press.

DRAMA

48 RHODE ISLAND FEMINIST THEATRE. <u>Internal Injury</u>. Providence,
   R.I.: RIFT, 1978.
   This play explores in a serious way the stories of three
   battered women. Depicts each woman's point of view through
   monologue, scenes of the past and present, and choral pas-
   sages. Each woman assumes the role of secondary character
   and a part in the chorus. Production rights will be re-
   leased when the play leaves the repertory. Currently available for touring nationwide. For more information, contact:
   Booking Committee, RIFT, Box 9083, Providence, R.I. 02940.
   Telephone (401) 273-8654.

HISTORICAL PERSPECTIVES

49 GAYFORD, J. J. "Battered Wives One Hundred Years Ago."
   <u>The Practitioner</u> 219, no. 1309 (July 1977):122-28.
   Presents historical view of the probable origin of the
   erroneous belief that wife battering was lawful since the
   woman was her husband's property. Also looks at the treatment of offenders. Cites views of nineteenth-century
   authors, including Dickens.

50 WOOLLEY, SABRA F. <u>Battered Women: A Summary</u>. Washington,
   D.C.: Women's Equity Action League, 1978, unpaged.
   A concise account of the recent history of an old problem.
   Includes the social context of wife abuse, causes, and laws.
   The Women's Equity Action League is located at 805 15th St.
   N.W., Washington, D.C. 20005.

LEGISLATIVE, JUDICIAL, AND POLICE ATTITUDES

51 BANNON, J. "Law Enforcement Problems with Intra-family Violence." Mimeographed. Detroit Police Department 1975.
    Police avoid domestic disputes, which they do not know how to resolve and which they view as the problems of individuals, not as a public issue. Explains extreme paradox of delegating the role of arbiters in family disputes to police officers, who are the most thoroughly socialized into masculine roles. As long as women are considered property, the outlook for better treatment is dim. The Constitution of the United States reflected the socialization of its framers: Women, as noncitizens, were not entitled to the protections extended to fully vested male citizens. Outlines an entirely new approach to training officers in conflict-intervention techniques.

52 EISENBERG, A. D. "Overview of Legal Remedies for Battered Women." *Trial* 15, no. 8 (August 1979):28-31.
    Eisenberg discusses the merits and disadvantages of several legal options available to abused wives who want to fight back against an abusing husband. He says that most judges favor the restraining order (also called a protective order), which is issued to an abuser ordering him to stay away from his wife, or simply to abstain from offensive conduct. Such stringent sanctions as a six-month prison term for non-compliance are in themselves a deterrent. Moreover, the order is immediately enforceable through a certificate of issuance delivered to the person to be protected, entitling the holder, in the event of violation, to the assistance of a police officer. Further, the police officer himself is protected by being provided with a civil warrant for swift action. He may take a violator into custody or take any other measure that will secure the protection that the order intends. And, finally, the order eliminates the need for intervention of any other court officer or of a social worker, or even for supplemental court proceedings.

53 FLEMING, JENNIFER B. Stopping Wife Abuse: A Guide to the Emotional, Psychological and Legal Implications for the Abused Woman and Those Helping Her. New York: Anchor/Doubleday, 1979, 532 pp. Bibliog.
    This comprehensive manual assumes that readers already know that wife abuse is a problem and seek to change the institutions with which the battered woman comes into contact. The author is a founder of the Women's Resource Network, which provides training, consultation, and

Legislative, Judicial, and Police Attitudes

technical assistance to law-enforcement personnel, social
service practitioners, and the staff of family violence
programs. The manual embodies a concept unique to feminists: the insistence that one not be bound by traditional
helping methods. Considers alternate paths to improving
conditions for battered women. Treats this multifaceted
subject from the perspectives of battered women and the
legal system. Discusses ways to influence legislation, the
variety of counseling techniques, and establishment of new
services. Includes a list of programs providing services.
Also provides the address of the National Coalition Against
Domestic Violence to inform those involved in wife abuse
prevention of current materials and resources. Comments on
the underlying sexist bias in traditional research in psychiatry, psychology, social psychology, and social work,
whereby scholars pass along to each succeeding generation
the tendency to look for sources of a problem within the
individual. This diminishes women's faith in themselves
and tends to lead to the "learned helplessness" described
by Leonore Walker in The Battered Woman (entry 75). Ency-
clopedic volume based upon the author's extensive experience. Along with Walker's book, may signal a breakthrough
in eliminating domestic violence.

54   FLYNN, J. P. "Recent Findings Related to Wife Abuse." Social
     Casework 58, no. 1 (January 1977):13-20.
          Summarizes a report of a research project on spouse
     assault conducted in Kalamazoo, Michigan, during May and
     June 1975 by a team of graduate students and faculty mem-
     bers of the School of Social Work of Western Michigan Uni-
     versity at the request of the Kalamazoo chapter of the
     National Organization for Women (NOW). Describes usual
     complicitous silence of community agencies with blame
     placed on the victim rather than the perpetrator by police,
     hospital staff, physicians, and attorneys.

55   LANGLEY, ROGER and LEVY, RICHARD. Wife Beating: The Silent
     Crisis. New York: E. P. Dutton, 1977, 252 pp. Bibliog.
          Explores dimensions of wife beating through legal and
     social history and data collected by sociologists, crimi-
     nologists, psychologists, and other researchers.

56   MARTIN, DEL. Battered Wives. San Francisco: Glide Publica-
     tions, 1976, 269 pp. Bibliog.
          Martin is a leading authority on the problem of battered
     wives and coordinator of Task Force on Battered Women of
     NOW. Argues foundation of problem not in husband/wife
     interaction or immediate triggering events but in the

Legislative, Judicial, and Police Attitudes

institution of marriage, historical attitudes toward women, the economy, and inadequacies in legal and social service systems. Recommends police and prosecutor's functions be constrained. Proposes specific legislation prohibiting wife abuse. Suggests that judges protect the wife by incarcerating the man rather than putting him on probation and deemphasizing reconciliation. Also suggests gun control, equal rights, and marriage contract legislation.

57 UNITED STATES CONGRESS. HOUSE COMMITTEE ON EDUCATION AND
    LABOR. Domestic Violence: Hearings, 16-17 March, on
    H.R. 7927 and H.R. 8948, to Authorize the Secretary of
    Health, Education, and Welfare to Establish a Grant Program
    to Develop Methods of Prevention and Treatment Relating to
    Domestic Violence, and for Other Purposes (95th Cong., 2nd
    Session). Washington, D.C.: Government Printing Office,
    1978, 753 pp.
        Text of bills H.R. 7927 and H.R. 8948 and testimony on
    domestic violence by sponsors, academic researchers, and
    workers in the field.

58 _____. Hearings on Domestic Violence: Prevention and
    Services. 10 and 11 July 1979 (96th Cong., 1st Session).
    Washington, D.C.: Government Printing Office, 1979.
        In support of H.R. 2977 (Mikulski-Muller Domestic Vio-
    lence Bill), which the House passed, volume of testimony
    by professionals dealing with domestic abuse in many dif-
    ferent but related fields: law, social work, criminal
    justice, and medicine. Recommends more effective training
    of personnel at the community level, more and better re-
    sources for victims, and relaxation of unrealistic eligibil-
    ity requirements, which make it difficult to provide
    existing resources and services to victims.

59 WISCONSIN LEGISLATIVE COUNCIL STAFF. SPECIAL COMMITTEE ON
    DOMESTIC VIOLENCE. "Issues Relating to Domestic Violence"
    (Discussion Paper 77-1), 1977. Bibliog.
        Defines domestic violence. Discusses development of
    data. Summarizes enacted and pending legislation in the
    United States. Identifies causes and presents possible
    solutions. Includes annotated bibliography.

60 WOODS, LAURIE. "Litigation on Behalf of Battered Women."
    Women's Rights Law Reporter 5 (Fall 1978):7-33.
        Describes a landmark lawsuit against the New York City
    police department and family court employees on behalf of
    battered women (Bruno v. Codd). Covers factual preparation
    and legal strategy. Includes the consent judgment against

27

the police department and the reasoning of the appellate
court in granting the court employees' motion to dismiss.
Demonstrates "that there is potential for successful litigation against the police, clerical employees of the courts,
and district attorneys, on behalf of battered women. . . .
Most importantly, their resolutions can carry enforceable
guarantees that the pattern and practice of leaving battered
women to fend for themselves within a sexist law enforcement
system, can be ended, albeit slowly and reluctantly."

MEDICAL ASPECTS

61 FLITCRAFT, ANNE. "Battered Women: An Emergency Room
    Epidemiology with a Description of a Clinical Syndrome and
    Critique of Present Therapeutics." Thesis, Yale Medical
    School. 1977, 45 pp. Bibliog.
        Unusual study by a woman physician who recognizes wife-
    beating as being of epidemic proportions. Understands the
    shortcomings of emergency room treatment, which traps bat-
    tered women into the pattern of more violence and self-
    destructive behavior by dismissing them as "hypochondriacs,
    hysterics or neurotics and again treated with minor tran-
    quilizers or psychiatric referrals." See entry 62 for a
    larger study based upon this pilot study.

62 STARK, EVAN; FLITCRAFT, ANNE; and FRAZIER, WILLIAM. "Medicine
    and Patriarchal Violence: The Social Construction of a
    'Private' Event." International Journal of Health Services
    9, no. 3 (1979):461-494.
        A further elaboration of the thesis advanced in entry 61.
    Verifies the thesis that the medical profession tends to
    trap women in circumstances from which they need to escape.
    Situates the medical profession's response to battered
    women's trauma within the political and economic arena
    where medicine operates as part of an extended patriarchy.

PSYCHOLOGICAL PERSPECTIVES

63 DWORKIN, ANDREA. "The Bruise That Doesn't Heal." Mother
    Jones 3 (July 1978):31-36.
        Poignant reminiscence of years as a battered woman by an
    articulate woman writer who can forget the physical pain

but not the painful emotions. Describes what it is like to be a survivor and how "in her life both a celebrant and proof of women's capacity and will to survive, to become, to act, to change self and society. And each year she is stronger and there are more of her."

64   GELLES, RICHARD J. "Abused Wives: Why Do They Stay?" Journal of Marriage and the Family 38, no. 4 (November 1976): 659-68.
     The fewer the resources and the less power the wife has, the more "entrapped" in her marriage and the more she suffers without calling for help.

65   HANKS, SUSAN E. "Battered Women: A Study of Women Who Live With Violent Alcohol-Abusing Men." American Journal of Orthopsychiatry 47, no. 2 (April 1977):291-306.
     Studies repeated violence by alcoholic husbands against spouses. Identifies three distinct types of family of origin. Suggests that women are influenced by family background in their responses to violence. Recommends that clinicians know background in order to help battered women to understand and to modify behavior.

66   PIZZEY, ERIN, and BLADES, ROGER. "Violence in the Family." Medico-Legal Journal 45, no. 3 (1977):65-81.
     An account of the varied responses of women who leave violent homes to live in a shelter providing a community of battered women. Clear evidence of "generational imprinting" described by Laing in Politics of the Family; that is, "We can trace in many of our mothers that violence back generations and you could see children getting imprinted as they came through." Describes work with the violent children of battered women: "The most extraordinary thing is that the children . . . are all good children because they are doing what their parents have told them; they are acting in a particular fashion because that is the family they have come from."

67   PRICE, JOHN, and ARMSTRONG, JEAN. "Battered Wives: A Controlled Study of Predisposition." Australian and New Zealand Journal of Psychiatry 12, no. 1 (March 1978):43-48.
     In this experiment, the researchers attempted to isolate the factors in a family background, especially the relationship of the wife to her father, that accounted for the breakup of a violent marriage. Tested two groups of women. Control group had experienced poor relationships with alcoholic fathers and criticized their husbands' heavy drinking, which escalated the violence and, ultimately, dissolved the

Psychological Perspectives

marriage. In contrast, second group had had better relationships with their fathers and tolerated their husbands'
equally heavy drinking better. Raises the possibility
that husband/wife violence in some cases is provoked by
criticism specifically of drinking.

68 RENVOIZE, JEAN. <u>Web of Violence: A Study of Family Violence</u>.
    London and Boston: Routledge & Kegan Paul, 1978, 240 pp.
    Bibliog.
        Written in a rambling, anecdotal style, with traditional
    biases. Hardly a study. Author, not identified by pro-
    fessional affiliation but apparently a psychiatrist, is
    acquainted with all the aspects of intrafamily violence.
    Speaks of the "politics" of refuges for battered women.
    Prefers Pizzey's warm, outgoing, untidy shelter over the
    efficient, government-operated shelters that have been the
    outgrowth of her work.

69 ROUNSAVILLE, BRUCE J. "Theories in Marital Violence: Evidence
    From a Study of Battered Women." <u>Victimology</u> 3, no. 1-2
    (1978-1979):11-31.
        Promotes two types of theories to explain wife beating:
    psychological and sociological. Reveals important prac-
    tical consequences of adhering to any one perspective.
    Considers hypotheses in terms of data on battered women.
    Evidence supports all of social and psychological explana-
    tions offered in at least a portion of the sample, as well
    as the need for a "systems analysis" approach to the prob-
    lem, viewing family violence as the final, common pathway
    of multiple determinants. In particular, suggests the
    major characteristic of the syndrome of wife beating is
    the intense and exclusive dyadic system in which the couple
    is enmeshed. As individuals, the man may not be violent
    and the woman may be unwilling to tolerate abuse; once in
    the relationship, however, a dynamic is created in which
    violence occurs in a regular fashion.

70 ROUNSAVILLE, BRUCE J. et al. "Natural History of a Psycho-
    therapy Group for Battered Women." <u>Psychiatry</u> 42, no. 1
    (February 1979):63-78.
        The subjects of this study were battered women who first
    came to a hospital for treatment of physical complaints symp-
    tomatic of physical abuse. Through a questionnaire and
    screening, some of the women decided to enter a therapy
    group with other battered women. The author-psychiatrists
    devised a consciousness-raising program to address the
    special problems of battered women, which was first sup-
    portive and informative, later confrontational and

interpretive. Concede limited success because of (1) high dropout rate due to the stigma of being in a battered women's therapy group; (2) the presence of a male cotherapist; (3) the women's fear that the promise of help was flimsy; (4) unwillingness to scrutinize strong attachments to abusive relationships and to gratifying periodic reconciliations, combined with the threat involved in terminating relationships; and (5) probably the premature offer of psychological help to the women whose physical symptoms had been primary. Psychological treatment is only one of several necessary resources including more shelters for battered women and modifications in law and in welfare regulations so that unmarried couples may not be excluded from services.

71   STAR, BARBARA. "Comparing Battered and Non-Battered Women." *Victimology* 3, no. 1-2 (1978-1979):32-44.
        Contrasts specific psychosocial aspects in the lives of fifty-seven battered and nonbattered women who sought refuge at Haven House, a shelter in the Los Angeles area. Challenges the masochism theory. Identifies passivity, not the need for maltreatment, as the rationale for enduring physical abuse. Also analyzes the impact of education, religion, and early family environment. Calls for services for abused and abusers.

72   STAR, BARBARA et al. "Psychosocial Aspects of Wife Battering." *Social Casework* 60 (October 1979):479-87.
        To deal effectively with wife abuse, social workers need to know more about victims' personal and social traits. Empirical study presenting a psychosocial profile of battered women, with multistep therapeutic intervention. Besides a routine personal history, the data included the woman's history of exposure to violence and her sense of competence and strength in such areas as motherhood, interpersonal relations, and finances. The responses all indicated stress in these areas and revealed that counseling should include helping the abused woman learn the techniques of mastering her environment, feeling pride in independent accomplishments, being able to tolerate ambivalence, and finding suitable role models. Social workers can use their position as consistent, understanding adult figures to establish trusting relationships. For maximum effectiveness, therapeutic contact must extend beyond crisis treatment or brief respite at shelters and include long-term therapy through outreach programs and ongoing group sessions.

73   SYMONDS, ALEXANDRA. "Violence Against Women--The Myth of Masochism." *American Journal of Psychotherapy* 33, no. 2 (April 1979):161-73.

Battered Women

Psychological Perspectives

Symonds, a psychotherapist, finds a strong resemblance
between battered women and victims of other kinds of natural
and human catastrophes. Isolated victims of repeated brutality without outside support, women are infantalized as
are victims of brainwashing, floods, and earthquakes, as
well as inmates of concentration camps. A common reaction
in all these cases is panic, or sheer terror, which leads
to paralysis. Society and particularly psychotherapists
must reject the myth that women provoke violence. At last,
shelters for battered women offer the freedom from isola-
tion, which some women victims fear more than beatings.

74　SYMONDS, MARTIN. "The Psychodynamics of Violence-prone
　　Marriages." American Journal of Psychoanalysis 38, no. 3
　　(Fall 1978):213-22.
　　　　Symonds's special interest at the Karen Horney Clinic
　　and in private practice has been victimology. Maintains
　　that, although husbands are also abused, only wives are
　　severely crippled and feel terrorized. Distinguishes be-
　　tween and presents cases of violence, aggression, and
　　hostility--terms that are often used synonymously. Broadly
　　divides violent marriages into two major groups: (1)
　　those where the violence derives from preexisting character
　　structure of individuals, almost exclusively the husband's;
　　and (2) those where the violence is produced by conflicts
　　within the marital relationship. Violence here represents
　　a failure of communication between partners. Identifies
　　several abusive kinds of men. In certain long-term mar-
　　riages, counseling is of little help because the partners
　　are "welded together by vindictive helplessness." Counsel-
　　ing most effective when failure of communication has been
　　the major source of trouble: "Violence is the response of
　　despair when the listening stops and the war begins."

75　WALKER, LENORE E. The Battered Woman. New York: Harper &
　　Row, 1979, 270 pp.
　　　　Contends that psychological abuse is often more harmful
　　than physical abuse. Study of data on both kinds of coer-
　　civeness is divided into three parts. Part 1, "Psychology
　　of the Battered Woman," describes and refutes the time-
　　honored stereotypical myths about the battered and the bat-
　　terer that have prevented our recognition of battered women
　　as victims. Part 2, "Coercive Techniques in Battering
　　Relationships," discusses how all kinds of abuse (physical,
　　sexual, and economic) disrupt family life. Presents and
　　reiterates her theory of violence as having three distinct
　　phases: tension-building, explosion into acute battering,
　　and the follow-up "loving" respite. Part 3, "The Way Out,"

examines the legal, medical, psychological, and other means
of keeping battered women as victims. Observes that currently help for victims is becoming a national priority
with studies at all levels of government. Prescriptive
and descriptive, sketches three-level intervention system
to develop new services and strengthen existing resources.
Feels that Pizzey's safe house at Chiswick, England, the
derivatives throughout England, and the equivalents in the
United States are models for providing a sense of community,
a support system, and a beginning of women's realization
that they have the power to change their lives. The cool
social scientist and the compassionate feminist share the
conviction that the traditional idea of a family unit must
be relinquished, for it does not now and never can provide
tranquility in the modern world.

SERVICES FOR BATTERED WOMEN

76   BASS, DAVID, and RICE, JANET. "Agency Responses to the
      Battered Wife." Social Casework 60 (June 1979):338-42.
         This study showed that most counselors did not know of
      community resources to assist the abused wife and attempted
      to deal with the problem in the same way they would handle
      other family problems. Because social work agencies empha-
      size interaction of the whole family counselors feel they
      can manage any situation, even though a joint effort by
      several agencies might be more beneficial.

77   BUSINESS AND PROFESSIONAL WOMEN'S FOUNDATION. "Battered Women."
      Info Digest. Washington, D.C.: Business and Professional
      Women's Foundation, 1978, 11 pp. offset.
         Foundation occasional paper on battered women. Succinct
      outline of the problem. Lists resources, services, and
      technical assistance available to address the problem. The
      Foundation is located at 2012 Massachusetts Ave., N.W.,
      Washington, D.C. 20036.

78   DAVIDSON, TERRY. Conjugal Crime: Understanding and Changing
      the Wife-Beating Pattern. New York: Hawthorn Books, 1978,
      274 pp. Bibliog.
         In author's family, father, a respected minister, ter-
      rorized his wife and children. Emphasizes from experience
      that family abuse is not a crime exclusively of the impov-
      erished. Discusses various means of support for battered
      families and means of preventing abuse.

Services for Battered Women

79   McSHANE, CLAUDIA. "Community Services for Battered Women."
      Social Work 24, no. 1 (January 1979):34-39.
          A leader in the Wisconsin network for battered women,
      McShane feels that traditional social workers need to have
      their consciousness raised, "altering professional roles
      and improving overall delivery of services." Also empha-
      sizes the importance of a community network system in
      maintaining communication among personnel and in improving
      continuity of services to battered women. Would also allow
      for the exchange of staff among agencies, joint opportunity
      for staff development, mutual contractual arrangements and
      securing of resources. Such changes would reduce fragmenta-
      tion of services to the battered woman and most effectively
      direct her to the services she needs. For professionals
      working with battered women, recommends workshops on such
      essentials as law enforcement and legal and medical regu-
      lations to dispel prevailing myths. In short, a network of
      professionals working closely with police and women's
      groups could improve overall services to battered women.

SOCIOLOGICAL INQUIRIES

80   CHIMBOS, PETER D. Marital Violence: A Study of Interpersonal
      Homicide. San Francisco, Calif.: R & E Research Asso-
      ciates, Inc., 1978, 109 pp. Bibliog.
          Sociological inquiry into thirty-four recent husband/
      wife homicides in Canada. Provides relevant information
      on violent behavior and on the influence of various social
      and sociopsychological factors upon family behavior. Stud-
      ied the respondents' early childhood experiences of physical
      punishment, previous marital conflict, and the situational
      pressures surrounding the homicide. Does not claim his
      study is representative of the whole population, based as
      it is upon a limited number of cases. In his review of the
      literature, claims to have filled in some of the research
      gaps in previous studies of lethal violence in the family.
      Final chapter discusses prospects for prevention of inter-
      spousal homicide.

81   DOBASH, R. EMERSON, and DOBASH, RUSSELL. Violence Against
      Wives. New York: The Free Press, 1979, 339 pp. Bibliog.
          This scholarly work by two Scottish professionals and
      activists in the field of domestic violence demystifies all
      the patriarchal shibboleths of wife beating. The current
      term "domestic violence," designed to democratize the

language and make it applicable to both sexes, also neutral-
izes the impact and makes it less reprehensible in the public eye, for the term implies that men and women are equally
culpable in committing violent acts. Not so. The authors'
concern is, specifically, brutality against women, the victims from earliest times. Intends to make the reader aware
of wife abuse in its full social and cultural context by
bringing together accounts of the social control and abuse
of women from numerous standard historical sources. Chap-
ters on the helping professions and police and legal response also reveal the power of myth in dealing with
(disguising) wife abuse. Extensive bibliography of recent
and older works.

82   GELLES, RICHARD J. The Violent Home: A Study of Physical
      Aggression between Husbands and Wives. Sage Library of
      Social Research, vol. 13. Beverly Hills, Calif.: Sage
      Publications, 1974, 230 pp. Bibliog.
          According to author, exploratory, inconclusive study
      based upon eighty interviews. Reaches certain inescapable
      conclusions: The family, more than any other social insti-
      tution, is the primary mechanism for teaching norms, values,
      and techniques of violence and is far more basic than is
      violence on television or school discipline; violence is
      learned behavior.

83   NICHOLS, BEVERLY B. "The Abused Wife Problem." Social Case-
      work 57, no. 1 (January 1976):27-32.
          Says that old-fashioned rigidity of patriarchal social
      system limits innovation in treatment of abused wives.
      Caseworkers philosophically linked to preservation of
      family life are reticent to give real help to victims.
      Moreover, minority group traditions accept wife abuse as
      a fact of life. More professional social workers from
      minority groups are needed to deal with the serious problems
      that ethnicity creates. Thus far, only the Women's Move-
      ment has seen through stereotypes and initiated innovative
      approaches to treatment of abuse.

84   STACHURA, JAMES B., and TESKE, JR., R. H. C. "A Special
      Report on Spouse Abuse in Texas." Huntsville, Texas:
      Sam Houston State University Criminal Justice Center,
      Survey Research Program, 1979, 18 pp.
          According to the authors, this is possibly a unique study
      in that it used mail survey methods to gauge the extent of
      the problem of spouse abuse and its severity. Based upon
      the responses of 682 Texans, the survey established for the
      first time a firm base for future research by providing

information on the nature and scope of conjugal violence in
the state of Texas. No fewer than 87,000 persons in the
adult population are subject to spouse abuse on at least
a weekly basis. All income levels are involved, and the
proportion is the same among whites, blacks, and Mexican-
Americans.

85 STAHLY, GERALDINE BUTTS. "A Review of Select Literature of
Spousal Abuse." Victimology 2, no. 3-4 (1977-1978):591-607.
Contends from extensive review of the literature that
the theory of family violence is considerably ahead of the
empirical analysis needed to support and verify it. Discusses at length the content of several theoretical approaches to spousal abuse literature, particularly research
papers on spousal assault in a social-structural context.
Demonstrates to what extent more additional empirical
research is needed.

86 STEINMETZ, SUZANNE K. "The Battered Husband Syndrome."
Victimology 2, no. 3-4 (1977-1978):499-509.
Uses historical data, comic strips assumed to reflect
popular values, and data derived from several empirical
studies. Examines the phenomenon of husband-battering,
which Steinmetz claims has occurred as long as wife-
battering, although husbands fail to report the crime in
most cases. In seventy-three percent of the comic strips,
wives were more aggressive; in ten percent, husbands and
wives were equally aggressive; and in seventeen percent,
males were more aggressive. Suggests that comics reflect
family life and lifestyles and reinforce family-related
behavior. Criticized severely by feminists as an almost
totally inaccurate interpretation of the facts, full of
specious arguments, and an egregious disservice to the
Women's Movement in terms of the effectiveness of its work
with battered women.

87 _____. The Cycle of Violence: Assertive, Aggressive, and
Abusive Family Interaction. Praeger Special Studies in
U.S. Economic, Social and Political Issues. New York:
Praeger 1977, 191 pp. Bibliog.
Interview with fifty-seven intact urban and suburban
families from a wide range of economic and ethnic groups
and geographic areas. Based upon answers to a questionnaire and diaries of daily intrafamily events. The respond-
ents thus became part of the research team. Intended to
provide baseline data on patterns of intrafamily conflict
resolution and on how typical American families deal with
the stress of marriage and family life and survival. From

consideration of the results, evolved a typology of family
conflict-resolving modes that identified four distinct
types: "screaming sluggers, silent attackers, threateners,
and pacifists." The conditions that foster family violence,
such as unemployment, inadequate role fulfillment, insecur-
ity, lack of family- or community-support systems, and iso-
lation are also found in the backgrounds of those who commit
other acts of violence. A study similar to this and with
which Steinmetz was involved is Straus's Behind Closed
Doors: Violence in the American Family, based upon 2,143
families. Suggests that perhaps the question to be asked
is not "How can we change family interaction?" but rather
"Are we willing to change the social structure?" May be
dysfunctional to train children to be nonaggressive and
nonviolent in a social system that requires competition
and aggressiveness for social survival.

88   STRAUS, MURRAY A.   "Sexual Inequality, Cultural Norms, and
     Wife-Beating." Victimology 1, no. 1 (Spring 1976):54-70.
         Identifies nine specific ways in which the male-dominant
     structure of society and family creates and maintains a
     high level of marital violence. Also contains many good
     references.

89   STRAUS, MURRAY A.; GELLES, RICHARD J.; and STEINMETZ,
     SUZANNE K. Behind Closed Doors: Violence in the American
     Family. Garden City, New York: Anchor Books, 1980,
     301 pp. Bibliog. Appendices.
         Most statistics and discussions of the facts are con-
     tained in notes and appendices at the end, in order to
     make this study of 2,143 families readable by and under-
     standable to a large audience. Conclusions and prescrip-
     tions, especially in terms of current political and economic
     situation, are idealistic (unrealistic), but must be con-
     sidered. "Stopgap," "bandaid," treatment of violence is
     ultimately meaningless. Family life will continue to be
     the source of misery for millions of people unless (1) the
     norms that legitimate and glorify violence in society are
     eliminated; (2) violence-provoking stresses created by
     society--joblessness, loss of self-respect and ability to
     cope with stress, and inadequate health care--are halted;
     (3) families are integrated into a network of kin and com-
     munity to reduce isolation and alienation; and (4) the
     sexist character of society and family, with the concept
     of "women's work" being less important and lower-paid, is
     done away with.

Sociological Inquiries

90   TIDMARSH, MANNES. "Violence in Marriage: The Relevance of
      Structural Factors." Social Work Today 7, no. 2
      (4 April 1976):36-38.
         Examines available evidence to identify causes of bat-
      tering and finds that while no two cases are alike, there
      are many common factors: social isolation without a social
      safety valve, wives' embarrassment in talking over their
      situation with relatives, relationship between drunkenness
      and violence, immaturity of young couples, overcrowding,
      financial strain, poor accommodations. Believes that the
      current move toward greater equality in a short time also
      leads to greater violence. Ultimately, the flexibility
      of equality will reduce violence.

91   UNITED STATES COMMISSION ON CIVIL RIGHTS. Battered Women:
      Issues of Public Policy. Washington, D.C.: United States
      Commission on Civil Rights, 1978, 706 pp. Bibliog.
         Statements by participants in a "consultation" to dis-
      cuss the entire problem of brutality in the home. Included
      experts in the field of abuse from many disciplines, repre-
      senting also a diverse racial, ethnic, and geographic popu-
      lation. Objectives were "to identify sound, existing
      research data, as well as research gaps, and consequently,
      to consider research strategies; to identify necessary
      State legal and law enforcement reform; to identify needed
      short- and long-term support services for battered women;
      to identify, in all of the above, the appropriate Federal
      role; to facilitate communication among researchers, activ-
      ists, policymakers, and others; and to inform the public."

92   WOLFGANG, MARVIN E. "Family Violence and Criminal Behavior."
      Bulletin of the American Academy of Psychiatry and the Law
      4, no. 4 (1976):316-27.
         Concludes that "violence in the family is partly a
      reflection of violent expression in the culture generally.
      But serious crimes within the family are most commonly
      related to sub-cultural values that minimally do not much
      inhibit physical responses or maximally condone and encour-
      age them." Expresses the subculture of violence theory.

93   "Working With Battered Women: A Conversation with Lisa
      Leghorn." Victimology, 3, no. 1-2 (1978-1979):91-107.
         In a wide-ranging exchange, Leghorn tells Viano, editor
      of Victimology, that not having a paying job and thus being
      economically dependent on her husband and powerless intensi-
      fies the plight of the abused wife. The wife does not have
      sufficient control over her life to leave when she has been
      brutalized. On the inadequacies of traditional police
      response, Leghorn described her in-service teaching at

Boston Police Academy. Police tend to perpetuate all the clichés that women's verbal abuse is the impetus that justifies beating. Even when doing what the law requires, police are still sympathetic to the husband.

SPECIAL JOURNAL ISSUES

94 Social Work 21, no. 6 (November 1976):418-91.
        Special issue on women. Two articles, "Helping Victims of Rape" and "Battered Wives: An Emerging Social Problem," discuss the need to raise the consciousness of agency staffs and the role of advocacy in abuse.

95 "Spouse Abuse." Social Action and the Law 4, no. 6 (July 1978). Brooklyn, New York: Brooklyn College, Center for Responsive Psychology.
        Special issue on domestic violence in the journal of the Center for Responsive Psychology. Three articles and four book reviews describe the legal implications of jury selection, courtroom tactics, and police intervention. Aspires "to present both the advocates' positions and data from research aimed at giving insight into community attitudes about domestic violence. We hope these data will give social scientists some basis for sharpening theory, advocates insights into the type and prevalence of attitudes they will wish to change, as well as the most appropriate targets, and attorneys help in reviewing and revising strategies." Issue may be obtained for $1.50 from the Center in Brooklyn, New York 11210.

96 "Spouse Abuse." Victimology: An International Journal 2, no. 3-4 (1977-1978).
        Issue devoted to articles on various aspects of spouse abuse by a number of well-known theorists whose other writings are widely read. Contributors include E. Dobash and Russell P. Dobash, Murray A. Straus, Elaine Hilberman, Fran P. Hosken, Suzanne K. Steinmetz, and Leonore E. Walker. Several respondents challenge the statistics and interpretations in Steinmetz's controversial article, "The Battered Husband Syndrome" (see entry 86). They deplore the fact that funding by the National Institute of Mental Health gives credibility to her arguments in newspapers worldwide and in congressional hearings on domestic violence legislation. Her work gives fuel to the backlash against the Women's Movement. In at least one case, money to open a shelter for battered women was withheld on the basis of Steinmetz's writings.

Chapter 3
Rape

The subjects of rape and battered women are related chronologically. This relationship is manifest in the research into their histories and causes and in the practical measures for improving the way that victims are treated by police and by medical and court personnel. Rape crisis centers, hot lines, advocacy groups, and shelters became realities almost simultaneously. Research has insisted upon reform through publicizing how widespread violence really is.

At the federal level, Congress enacted legislation to fund research on rape and establish the National Center for the Prevention and Control of Rape within the National Institute of Mental Health in April 1976. The Center supports research and research demonstration to understand sexual assault, refine prevention and treatment strategies, and implement public policies and practices.

Rapists and Wife Beaters: Who They Are
It is generally agreed that the seeds of any form of violence are planted in the home, where the most important part of socialization occurs. Children who either see violence between parents or are victims are more likely to become batterers or victims than those who never see their parents abused or are not subjected to corporal punishment. Gender-role stereotyping, when taught and reinforced at an early age, makes boys become more aggressive than girls. In the male subculture, females are virtually always treated as inferior, weak, and passive. Fairy tales, cartoons, television programs, and commercials all reinforce this image. The pastor of a Lutheran Church in Portage, Wisconsin summed up machismo in this description of a man who had recently murdered his wife, two children, and himself: "He was what has come to be known as the typical 'macho' male, he believed he wasn't supposed to have any problems . . . that he wasn't supposed to share his problems. He really felt he had to be in control" (Wisconsin State Journal, Madison, 21 February 1979).

Donna D. Schram ("Rape," in entry 1), p. 55, says that it is difficult to draw a consistent picture of a rapist. Rapists have been variously described as antisocial, psychopathic, autistic,

depressed, less intelligent than other convicted felons--but also as
being of average or above-average intelligence--as good treatment
prospects--and also as poor treatment prospects. Schram believes
it is inaccurate to suggest that rapists have common characteristics.
There are more similarities than differences between rapists and non-
rapists. All in all, she finds a confusing variety of views. Moreover, ninety-seven percent of offenders are never apprehended and
therefore never participate in any research defining their characteristics. The remaining three percent hardly constitute an adequate
sample. Nevertheless, research continues.

Psychiatrist M. L. Cohen and his associates, in "The Psychology
of Rapists" (entry 97), pp. 291-314, offer a reasonable assessment
based upon what appear to be three types of rapists differentiated
by their underlying motivation. Those men with an "aggressive aim,"
skilled and attractive, have a good prognosis for recovery. A second
type with a "sexual aim" also appears to have a good prognosis for
recovery; however, treatment is long-term and there are many regres-
sions. Members of a third type, "sexual aggression-diffusion," display such capacity for brutality and sadism that they do not benefit
from treatment.

Martin Symonds, director of the Victimology Program at the Karen
Horney Clinic, confirms the view that rapists, whether compulsive or
predatory, psychologically terrorize their victims and act in a
physically violent and sadistic way to achieve immediate control
over them (entry 129), pp. 27-34.

Sexism and the Law
Probably nowhere else has language so influenced society's attitude toward violence as in the wording of laws concerning rape.
These were based upon traditional mores governing sexual relations.
They did not protect women as individuals but rather as the property
of men. Nor have legal commentators shown great sensitivity in
interpreting the law. No man, except a male prisoner who has been
raped, can understand women's fear of rape. These are the conten-
tions of Camille E. LeGrand, whose study published in Forcible Rape:
The Crime, the Victim, and the Offender, entry 97, dates from 1973.
The outrage felt by activists in the Women's Movement has spurred
considerable change since that time. Laws still vary a good deal
by state. New York, California, Michigan, and Wisconsin are among
the thirty-six states that have eased the rules of evidence that in
the past have made it difficult to prosecute a rape case sucessfully
and have traumatized the victim by making it appear that she, not the
rapist, was on trial.

Attorney LeGrand has been especially discerning in her study of
the history of rape law, emphasizing its overprotectiveness of the
female in its regard for her as man's property, its use of words
like ravaging and despoiling. She shows how California formerly

categorized rape as a crime against public decency and good morals, along with horse racing, gambling, indecent exposure, and abortion. Until recently, California had never viewed rape as a crime against one's physical integrity, peace of mind, or freedom of movement without fear of attack.

LeGrand describes in detail what police departments everywhere have named unfounded complaints. "This term," she says, "is a technical one, meaning only that police, for various reasons, have decided not to advise prosecution. It does not imply that a woman's report of the rape is inaccurate. The unfortunate ambiguity of the term and the high rate of 'unfounding' have probably contributed to the myth that women make many false rape complaints."

The following are examples of reasons given for unfounded complaints. The victim was intoxicated. She delayed in reporting. There is nothing in her physical condition to support the allegation. She refuses to submit to a medical examination. The victim knew the offender. A weapon was used to threaten her, but there was no actual battery.

There is no mention that victims may be young, afraid, and too embarrassed to cooperate with the police investigation. Once a complaint is termed "unfounded," there is no chance of obtaining a conviction in court.

There are still other reasons for dismissing a rape complaint. One is "victim precipitation," a phrase coined first by Amir, an Israeli criminologist. He meant that the victim had behaved in a manner to suggest or to signal to the offender that she consented to sexual relations and thus made herself vulnerable. The concept of victim precipitation derives from male definitions of expressed or implied consent and therefore restricts what a female is allowed to do. She should neither walk in dark areas alone nor hitchhike. The view that men hold of sexual invitation is clearly unreasonable. Yet it is so ingrained in society's thinking that women accept the definition and feel guilty about their decisions to do or not to do certain things. In short, victim precipitation is nothing more than a male view of events preceding the incident.

A medical examination of the victim may give evidence for her complaint of rape; however, police often have not used medical evidence available to them.

Myths are other obstacles that a victim confronts. Thus, women are considered hostile or immoral. They seek to convict innocent men. Women like to be raped (a dictum attributed by Susan Brownmiller [entry 32], p. 315 to Helene Deutsch, a follower of Freud). Men are at the mercy of uncontrollable emotions.

The hurdles multiply. The victim has to submit to a psychological examination or a lie detector test to demonstrate that she is not subject to delusions. Having been put on trial before the courtroom trial, she then has to undergo the resistance standard: Did she or did she not resist her assailant who was holding a gun or a knife to her head? What were her previous (nonmarital) sexual experiences? Yet the offender is never asked such questions. Finally, the judge cautions the jury: Remember that you may convict an innocent man. As LeGrand remarks, the criminal justice system's desire to protect good, chaste, young women clashes with its fear of convicting an innocent man, one of their own.

Today, mercifully, many of these blatant abuses have been eliminated. Much of the literature does reflect fairer attitudes toward the handling of the crime. Between 1973 and 1976, new rape legislation was enacted in thirty-six states and proposed in thirteen others.

In general, there have been two types of change: adoption of new and wider definitions of rape and a relaxation of proof requirements. The tendency is now to identify the crime as criminal sexual assault, thereby making it sex-neutral and applicable to both women and men.

Response of the Women's Movement to the Trauma of Abuse

Lisa Leghorn has identified three parallels in the history of the movements against wife-abuse and against rape: their analysis of the source of violence against women; their description of the traditional response to violence against women by the criminal justice system and social and governmental agencies; and the nature of the grassroots response (entry 91), p. 449. In both movements, "the grassroots groups have exposed the nature of power relations between men and women and the institutions that sustain those relations. They have also developed an alternative, self-help response that has been so effective that it has been imitated by some of the very same institutions that had formerly been so antagonistic to victims of rape and wife abuse." Leghorn further voices the concern of these grassroots groups that have been dealing with rape victims and family abuse situations. These groups should be recognized and funded so that their work can continue. Their intimate knowledge and understanding of the problem are invaluable resources in the growing efforts to seek solutions.

The many cities in which women have now conducted "Take Back the Night" marches, "No More Assaults" months, and comparable demonstrations against sexual harassment and pornography have magnified public awareness and concern. Women have produced films, dramas, and other effective learning materials. They have instituted educational programs in schools and churches and at other forums. The number and focus of conferences across the country are too many to count. Sensitive media treatment has also increased.

Two women who responded simultaneously to rape victims' needs for practical assistance and provided victim-related research are Ann Wolbert Burgess and Lynda Lytle Holmstrom (entry 97). They gave both crisis and long-term counseling to victims at Boston City Hospital's Emergency Room and were available whenever needed. Burgess, a psychiatric nurse, and Holmstrom, a sociologist, have documented a "rape trauma syndrome" with a distinct stage of acute pain, psychological and somatic reactions, mood changes, and an ultimate reintegrating of the experience into the victim's life. They have also described different forms of rape. They distinguish between sudden attacks and those that occur after the assailant first insinuates himself into the confidence of the victim. Both women maintain that rape victims experience predominantly fear of injury, mutilation, and death—not guilt or shame. They have revealed how much insensitive postrape treatment by hospital personnel and police contributes to the trauma of the victim.

One particularly insightful case study that confirms and dramatizes the findings of Burgess and Holmstrom is a personal account by Deena Metzger (entry 122). A fiction writer, poet, and psychotherapist, Metzger was the victim of a brutal rape. She has retold that experience and the subsequent long trauma, not so much as a cool research report, but rather as an essay on a devastating life event, the account of which is visceral in its grip. This experience clearly depicts the many-faceted, long-range needs of rape victims.

Studies of rape crisis centers also abound. Donna D. Schram ("Rape," in entry 1), pp. 53-79, identifies many different forms that both counseling and advocacy services assume; for example, crisis lines with volunteers available around-the-clock, who have had training in crisis intervention, rape law, and criminal procedure. Also available are the traditional mental health counselors who rely upon long-term counseling and assure proper medical follow-up for the victim.

As an outgrowth of these efforts, victims and advocates note considerable progress in the several institutions with which rape victims come into contact: the police, the medical establishment, and the criminal justice system. Better police/community relations, training of police to handle rapes, and the increased number of women on police forces have resulted in more sensitive police behavior in many communities. Similar advances are found in the courts, where district attorneys, prosecutors, and judges are increasingly attentive to the rights of victims and witnesses. This is especially true where sexual assault laws have been modernized and where formal advocates serve.

The chief complaints regarding medical treatment have been the indifference and lack of respect shown by personnel, their unwillingness to give victims information on the tests performed on them, and lack of privacy. As a result, the victim feels humiliated. Through the unremitting work of the Women's Movement, some hospitals have altered their treatment of victims. They have instituted training programs and issued written procedures to personnel. They have shared information on effective programs through membership in the National Coalition Against Sexual Assault and the National Organization of Victim Assistance. The member groups are increasingly successful in influencing public policy.

Sexual harassment does not necessarily include the act of physical rape. In that it often deprives a woman of her right to work and earn a living, sexual harassment may well be considered an act of psychological violence. This is especially true when that woman is also the sole support of her family. A survey conducted by the Working Women United Institute has defined sexual harassment as "any repeated and unwanted sexual comments, looks, suggestions on physical contact that you find objectionable or offensive and causes you discomfort on your job." Over the past several years several books, feminist newsletters (Spokeswoman), and popular women's magazines (Redbook) have treated this old problem, the latest area of abuse to become public knowledge. Courage to speak out and take action is now being supported not only by women's groups but also by top government officials (Patricia Harris, former Secretary of the Department of Health and Human Services, for example), city governments whose new ordinances make employers responsible for maintaining a work environment free from sexual harassment, and one of the nation's large labor unions (American Federation of State, City, and Municipal Employees), which published a booklet, Sexual Harassment: What the Union Can Do. This section includes material on "economic rape," a term designating sexual harassment on the job.

ANTHOLOGIES

97   CHAPPELL, DUNCAN, et al., eds. <u>Forcible Rape: The Crime,</u>
       <u>the Victim and the Offender</u>. New York: Columbia Univer-
       sity Press, 1977, 343 pp. Bibliog.
          Book of readings, some published for the first time,
       others reprinted. Griffin's "Rape: The All-American Crime"
       from <u>Ramparts</u> (1971) was the first extensive exploration of
       the subject from a feminist perspective. Eighteen articles
       from a number of disciplines: the law, sociology, psychol-
       ogy, medicine. Extensive bibliographies and references
       throughout. Contributors include names outstanding in the
       field, such as Ann Wolbert Burgess and Menachim Amir.

98   SCHULTZ, LEROY G., ed. <u>Rape Victimology</u>. Springfield, Ill.:
       Charles C. Thomas, 1975, 405 pp.
          Twenty articles from professional journals in criminol-
       ogy, sociology, law and medicine. Includes "The Victim in
       a Forcible Rape Case: A Feminist View" by Paula Lake Wood.
       Especially interesting is H. A. Snelling's "What Is Rape?"
       which explores ancient law on rape and punishment with
       pronouncements from the Roman, Jewish, and Anglo-Saxon law
       and such early legal writers as Coke, Hale, Hawkins, and
       Blackstone.

99   WALKER, MARCIA J., and BRODSKY, STANLEY L., eds. <u>Sexual</u>
       <u>Assault: The Victim and the Rapist</u>. Lexington, Mass.:
       Lexington Books, 1976, 186 pp. Bibliog.
          Anthology of readable studies on "institution" of rape
       from every point of view. Collected by the Rape Research
       Group, Psychology Department, University of Alabama. His-
       tory, criminal justice now and probable trends in the future,
       treatment of the victim and development of treatment centers,
       changing attitudes toward laws, preventive measures ini-
       tiated by the Women's Movement, treatment of rapists, and
       social definition are all included.

BIBLIOGRAPHIES

100 BARNES, DOROTHY L. <u>Rape: A Bibliography, 1965-1975</u>. Troy,
       New York: Whitson Publishing Co., 1977, 154 pp.
          Unannotated but inclusive bibliography. Contains many
       medical reports, for example, on the effects of child rape.

101 GEHR, MARILYN, comp. <u>Women as Victims of Violence: Battered</u>
       <u>Wives/Rape: Selected Annotated Bibliography</u>. Albany,

Bibliographies

N. Y.: SUNY, State Education Department, New York State
Library, Legislative Service, 1978, 23 pp.
   Originally prepared for the use of the New York State
legislature, surveys a variety of useful articles from the
1960s and early and mid-1970s. The latest date is 1977.
Emphasis upon law and legal procedures of various states.
Considers principally rape laws of the period.

102   KEMMER, ELIZABETH JANE. Rape and Rape-Related Issues: An
Annotated Bibliography. New York and London: Garland
Publishing Co., 1977, 174 pp.
   Detailed listing of studies between 1965 and 1976.
Covers the influence of media, medico-legal procedures,
offender characteristics, rape crisis centers, socio-
economic factors, and victim precipitation.

103   ST. LOUIS FEMINIST RESEARCH PROJECT. The Rape Bibliography:
A Collection of Abstracts. St. Louis, Mo.: Edy Netter,
1976, 96 pp.
   Includes entries from the 1940s. Covers legal, medical,
psychological, and sociological issues as well as material
from the popular press.

LEGISLATIVE, JUDICIAL, AND POLICE ATTITUDES

104   CLARK, LORENNE M. G., and LEWIS, DEBRA J. Rape: The Price of
Coercive Sexuality. Berkeley, Calif.: The Women's Press,
1978, 222 pp. Bibliog.
   Two feminist criminologists analyze 117 rape complaints
that were filed in Toronto, Canada, in 1970. They interpret
the data through their own theoretical model and conclude
that the judicial and educational systems require radical
structural change. The book includes notes and bibliography.

105   FULERO, SOLOMON M., and DELARA, CHRISTINE. "Rape Victims and
Attributed Responsibility: A Defensive Attribution
Approach." Victimology 1, no. 4 (Winter 1976):551-63.
   In two experiments, female subjects distinguished between rape victims to whom they were similar and dissimilar.
They attributed more responsibility to the latter. The
article discusses the influence of personal, preconceived
notions and extralegal attributes upon jurors. The data
support the "just world" theory that, where the solution
is problematic, the victim is accused of provocation.

Legislative, Judicial, and Police Attitudes

106   GEIS, GILBERT. "The Case of Rape: Legal Restrictions on
      Media Coverage of Deviance in England and America." In
      Deviance and Mass Media, vol. 2. Edited by C. Winick.
      Beverly Hills, Calif.: Sage Publications, 1978, 309 pp.
         The book is a collection of studies on media treatment
      of human afflictions, events, and experiences. Geis com-
      pares the legal restrictions imposed upon media coverage
      of rape in England and the United States. He discovers
      that the media system in England is less reticent about
      protecting the offender. The United States exhibits a well-
      established practice of discretion in publishing the names
      of rape victims. Many of the journalists who first covered
      rape trials were feminists who established media support
      for victims. Rape reform here was "an issue energizer."
      Yet maintaining anonymity of the victim makes rape a spe-
      cial kind of offense today. Geis suggests that anonymity
      camouflages the more fundamental issue, namely, that rape
      should be no different from other criminal offenses in
      which the offender is totally to blame.

107   GOTTESMAN, SHARON T. "Police Attitudes Toward Rape Before and
      After a Training Program." Journal of Psychiatric Nursing
      and Mental Health 15, no. 12 (December 1977):14-18.
         Training programs for police in several major cities
      addressed attitudes of police that, despite official re-
      sponsibility to protect victims and arrest rapists, often
      held the victim responsible. A survey showed that ninety-
      five percent of police officers responded positively to the
      training program and recommended further training in working
      with rape victims to increase recognition of the nature of
      rape trauma, awareness of personal feeling about rape and
      its effect upon the victim, and knowledge of hospital and
      legal procedures.

108   "Rape Visualization to Train Police." Innovations 4, no. 2
      (1977):30.
         In a discussion period and a role-playing interview with
      a victim after a dramatization of a rape scene, police
      officers differed in their responses from previous train-
      ing groups where rape visualization had not been shown.
      The visualization group exhibited far greater rage, but
      expressed none of the lewd comments of previous groups.

109   ROSE, VICKI M. "Rape as a Social Problem: A By-product of
      the Feminist Movement." Social Problems 25, no. 1
      (October 1977):75-89.
         The article carefully examines variations in current
      state laws pertaining to cross-examination, questions on

Legislative, Judicial, and Police Attitudes

the victim's previous sex life, probability of falsified claims, and civil libertarian opposition to circumscribing the defendant's ability to introduce the victim's sexual history into the case. The varying positions taken by civil libertarians depend upon whether they assume the victim's or the perpetrator's perspective.

110   SCHWARTZ, M. D., and CLEAR, T. R.   "Rape Law Reform and Women's Equality."   USA Today 108 (November 1979):35-37.
   The authors assert that one of the greater successes of the Women's Movement is convincing complacent, middleclass women that rape does not happen only to women of loose morals who "ask for it."   All women are potential victims. The authors review the treatment of rape in the courts and by society.   Men are assumed to need defense against "vindictive" women.   In effect, women are guilty until proven innocent.   The authors comment upon the improvement in Michigan's rape law, which, nevertheless, remains sexist in some respects.   Michigan and other states that have changed their rape laws still perpetuate the idea of women as a separate class of citizens through concern for their sexuality; this is inimical to full sexual equality.   "What is needed is not so much gender-neutral sex laws, but a sex-neutral criminal law.   The difference is both symbolic and operational."

111   SCROGGS, JAMES R.   "Penalties for Rape as a Function of Victim Provocativeness, Damage, and Resistance."   Journal of Applied Social Psychology 6, no. 4 (October-December 1976): 360-68.
   The experiment described revealed the existence of attitudes that may bias the equal administration of justice in cases of rape.   Penalties for the rapist are more severe if the victim is married rather than divorced.   If the victim is a virgin, the sentence is midway between that for raping a married woman and a divorcée.   The victim is "looking for it" if provocatively dressed or in a singles bar; both kinds of behavior are construed to indicate willingness. But rape is presumably different from other crimes, such as robbery, in which the victim offered no resistance.

MEDICAL ASPECTS

112   LeBOURDAIS, E.   "Rape Victims: The Unpopular Patients." Dimensions in Health Service 54, no. 3 (March 1976):12-14.

The article reports enlightened hospital treatment in a
Canadian hospital where traditional sexist attitudes of
male and female personnel toward victims had prevailed.
Ten recommendations could serve as a model for hospital
procedure.

113   McCOMBIE, SHARON L. et al. "Development of a Medical Center
      Rape Crisis Intervention Program." American Journal of
      Psychiatry 133, no. 4 (April 1976):418-21.
         A comprehensive study of a model hospital program dis-
      cusses the problems of implementation, including staff re-
      sistance, funding questions, and varying levels of
      counseling sophistication. The center has since become a
      resource center for the community.

114   McGUIRE, L. S., and STERN, MICHAEL. "Survey of Incidence of
      and Physicians' Attitudes Towards Sexual Assaults." Public
      Health Reports 91, no. 2 (March-April 1976):103-9.
         Quality of treatment of rape victims varies depending
      upon circumstances of the immediate follow-up care for the
      victim. Thus far, most of those dealing with rape victims
      right after the assault have been men with traditional male
      attitudes toward women.

115   MILLER, J. et al. "Recidivism Among Sexual Assault Victims."
      American Journal of Psychiatry 135, no. 9 (September 1978):
      1103-4.
         The University of New Mexico Medical School's Sexual
      Assault Response Team found that over a two and one-half
      year period eighty-two percent of 341 victims had been
      sexually assaulted before. The figure is probably higher
      than this limited survey shows. Some of their findings
      are as follows: the trauma of the current assault could
      not be resolved until prior assault(s) had been adequately
      addressed; an almost fatalistic attitude toward the current
      assault resulted from a long series of traumatic experi-
      ences; and a high proportion of unemployment among victims
      may reveal a link between poverty and being the victim of
      crime. For social, physical, or psychological reasons,
      victims may be less able to obtain or keep jobs, be less
      effective in their overall living patterns and thus easier
      prey to assault. Transiency may also be a factor. Rest-
      less, young runaways not yet street-wise are always at risk
      in depending upon strangers for food and shelter. Another
      factor is the greater prevalence of prior emotional dis-
      turbance, which suggests underlying vulnerability to sexual
      assault through naive trust and an inability to judge ex-
      ternal danger. Victims are more likely to have come from

broken homes. Strong dependency needs can be taken advantage of sexually and financially. Further avenues of exploration are whether recidivists are more likely than others to exhibit destructive behavior patterns.

PSYCHOLOGICAL PERSPECTIVES

116   BURGESS, ANN WOLBERT, and HOLMSTROM, LYNDA LYTLE. Rape: Crisis and Recovery. Bowie, Md.: Prentice Hall, Robert J. Brady, 1979, 477 pp.
      This work by the authors of earlier material on the treatment of rape victims in Boston is a longitudinal study of victims. It focuses upon victims' responses in crisis; effective counseling methods; and aids to recovery identified by victims. The book is divided into seven categories: Rape; Victim and Offender; Reactions to Rape; Community Reaction to Rape; Forensic Issues; Crisis Intervention; Counseling the Victim; and Recovery from Sexual Assault. Each chapter provides a detailed, step-by-step narrative of the procedures that victims and helping personnel are involved in from their first meeting to resolution of the case. Victims' statements in each phase of the postrape period illustrate the depth of trauma in sexual assault. The book also deals with treatment of child victims of incest. Chapter references and notes provide an additional resource.

117   _____. "Rape: Disclosure to Parental Family Members." Women and Health: The Journal of Women's Health Care 4, no. 3 (Fall 1979):255-68.
      The same team of researchers conducted this longitudinal study over four to six years from initial contact with a sample of rape victims. The study analyzes victims' reasons for or against disclosure of the rape to their parents. The majority of the eighty-one rape victims (forty-two percent) selectively told parents; thirty-three percent told all family members; and twenty-five percent told no family members. Victims' reasons for disclosure or nondisclosure ranged from wishing to protect their families from upsetting news, concern over value conflicts within their families, the desire to maintain independence, and the fact of psychological or geographical distance from their families. The article recommends that counselors help the victim predict family reaction to disclosure so that she make the right choice.

Rape

Psychological Perspectives

118   GROTH, A. NICHOLAS, and BIRNBAUM, H. JEAN. Men Who Rape:
       The Psychology of the Offender. New York: Plenum
       Publishing Co., 1979, 227 pp.
         The book is based upon Groth's clinical experiences with
       more than 500 rape offenders over a decade. It is divided
       into five chapters: Myths and Realities, Psychodynamics of
       Rape, Clinical Aspects of Rape, Patterns of Rape, and Guide-
       lines for Assessment and Treatment. Like nearly all pro-
       fessionals in the treatment of rapists, Groth pleads for
       the cooperation of all agencies, interaction of community
       services, and development of professional competence among
       service providers. He believes that one underlying theme
       pervades the early years of all rapists: sexual abuse or
       abuse in quasi- or nonsexual ways. Since not all abused
       children become rapists, however, lacking in rapists are
       the "civilizing influences . . . that mold the lives of
       non-rapists." The book is intended for a wide audience
       and all personnel who meet the rapist at some level in the
       prosecution process, that is, at rape crisis centers and
       as part of medical, religious, educational, legislative,
       and criminal justice systems.

119   GROTH, A. NICHOLAS, and BURGESS, ANN WOLBERT. "Rape: A
       Sexual Deviation." American Journal of Orthopsychiatry
       47, no. 3 (July 1977):400-406.
         The authors show that those who rape have failed to
       achieve an adequate sense of self-identity and self-worth.
       Mental health professionals have little opportunity to
       develop expertise in the treatment of the rapist because,
       if apprehended, he is punished as a felon rather than as a
       patient. The authors describe two motivations of rape
       (which share some characteristics): anger, in order to
       avenge rejection of the offender by women; and a desire
       for power, in order to mask rejection of the offender by
       the victim. Rape is a symptom of psychological disturbance
       that expresses conflict, defends against anxiety, and
       partially gratifies an impulse.

120   GROTH, A. NICHOLAS et al. "Rape: Power, Anger, and Sexuality."
       American Journal of Psychiatry 134, no. 11 (November 1977):
       1239-43.
         Accounts by offenders and victims of what occurs during
       a rape suggest that issues of power, anger, and sexuality
       are important in understanding the rapist's behavior. All
       three issues seem to be involved in each instance.

121   KATZ, SEDELLE, and MAZUR, MARY ANN. Understanding the Rape
       Victim. Series on Personality Processes. New York:
       John Wiley & Sons, 1979, 340 pp. Bibliog.

Psychological Perspectives

    The authors study the connection between rape and psy-
chiatric illness. Does rape precipitate and contribute to
psychiatric illness? Does illness precede rape and make
the victim more vulnerable to rape? In interviews with
eighty-four female psychiatric patients, over one-fourth
of those who had attempted suicide reported a past history
of rape. The authors concentrate on all forms of female
sexual victimization, including incest and child sexual
assaults. They review other empirical studies and deplore
the diversity of methodological design and the lack of
accurate statistics for any of these crimes. They uncover
resemblance between rape and other crimes against persons,
demographic similarity to victims of other kinds of crime,
profile characteristics of the offender, and high-risk
settings. They advocate better-designed research projects
that will promote a more significant understanding of the
rape victim, as well as successful programs of prevention.
The conclusion that rape occurs principally at the lower
end of the economic spectrum has been disproven in many
other studies. The authors reviewed an extensive bibliography of the literature for the present work.

122   METZGER, DEENA. "It Is Always the Woman Who Is Raped."
      American Journal of Psychiatry 133, no. 4 (April 1976):
      405-8.
         In a stunning analysis of a rape, the author-victim
      suggests that only in the community, through a kind of
      social ceremony that is similar to those associated with
      mourning and grief, can the victim recover the spirit that
      the rapist steals.

123   NOTMAN, MALKAH T., and NADELSON, CAROL C. "The Rape Victim:
      Psychodynamic Considerations." American Journal of
      Psychiatry 133, no. 4 (April 1974):408-13.
         The authors suggest that psychiatric help from a crisis
      intervention perspective rather than the usual, traditionally
      patriarchal psychiatric approach will support rape victims.
      The article describes likely reactions of three groups of
      rape victims--young, divorced or separated, and older women--
      and the kind of supportive counseling and reassurance needed
      for each type. Contains a selective bibliography.

124   RADER, CHARLES M. "MMPI Profile Types of Exposers, Rapists,
      and Assaulters in a Court Services Population." Journal of
      Consulting and Clinical Psychology 45, no. 1 (February 1977):
      61-69.
         This describes one of a number of Minnesota Multiphasic
      Personality Inventory (MMPI) experiments. The data support

the hypothesis that rapists who have committed offenses
involving both violence and sex indicate greater psychological disturbance than individuals committing offenses
involving either only sex (exposure) or only violence
(assaulters). A group profile of rapists shows them to
be irritable, hostile, angry, suspicious, somewhat depressed
and anxious, unpredictable, and peculiar in action and
thought. Repression, denial, fear of emotional involvement,
poor social intelligence, and serious difficulties in feeling empathy and communicating are other characteristics of
rapists.

125   SELIGMAN, CLIVE et al. "Rape and Physical Attractiveness:
       Assigning Responsibility to Victim." Journal of Person-
       ality 45, no. 4 (December 1977):554-63.
           Subjects of the experiment described assumed that un-
       attractive victims had been provocative, since the rapist
       would not voluntarily attack them. But in cases of mugging
       and robbery, the same subjects did not perceive attractive
       and unattractive victims differentially. The sexual con-
       notation must be removed from the crime of rape. Like any
       other physical assault, rape is an act of violence.

126   SELKIN, JAMES. "Protecting Personal Space: Victim and
       Resister Reactions to Assaultive Rape." Journal of
       Community Psychology 6, no. 3 (1978):263-68.
           Twenty-three victims of attempted rape and thirty-two
       victims of rape took two psychological inventory tests and
       filled out an interview form describing their feelings
       during the assault. The testing occurred days to years
       after the assault. The results of the tests and the inter-
       views showed that those participants, all volunteers, who
       identified themselves as resisters, were more confident,
       more socially adept, and angrier during the assault; they
       were even more actively resistant and freer of symptoms of
       emotional distress after the assault. Victims saw them-
       selves as emotionally and physically paralyzed, submissive
       and subdued. These results confirm the contention that
       women are trained to be rape victims and underline Susan
       Brownmiller's argument that women are culturally conditioned
       to be exploited. The study emphasizes the necessity of
       training women to resist.

127   SHAINESS, NATALIE. "Psychological Significance of Rape:
       Some Aspects." New York State Journal of Medicine 76,
       no. 12 (November 1976):2044-48.
           This study is one of the most pertinent on the causes of
       violence. Shainess cites both the Joanne Little and Inez

Psychological Perspectives

Garcia cases as examples of male insensitivity. There is
no true counterpart for rape in the male experience.
"Painful, dangerous, unwelcome invasion of the inner body
unknown to men . . . male homosexual anal rape is not a
reasonable equivalent." In addition, the presence of
weapons and the threat of brutality are unparalleled experiences. Whereas certain kinds of suffering may ultimately enrich a person's life, rape alters it completely
and in a less fortunate direction.

128 SILVERMAN, DANIEL. "First Do No More Harm: Female Rape
Victims and the Male Counselor." American Journal of
Orthopsychiatry 47, no. 1 (January 1977):91-96.
Male mental health workers must learn to be more
sensitive to rape victims, who are frequently referred to
them. The article considers the inherent difficulties
where the therapist is a man and discusses male misconcep-
tions and responses that might affect counseling.

129 SYMONDS, MARTIN. "The Rape Victim: Psychological Patterns of
Response." The American Journal of Psychoanalysis 36,
no. 1 (1976):27-34.
All rapists, whether compulsive or predatory, intimidate
and threaten acts of violence in order to subjugate the victim immediately. The victim reverts, naturally, to psychological infantilism when the gunman holds her at gunpoint,
deciding whether or not to kill her. To the outsider, this
behavior seems "friendly and cooperative." When rape is
viewed exclusively as a crime of violence, the victim's
behavior becomes understandable. The police become more
compassionate and less judgmental about behavior seen in
the context of extreme stress of sudden, unexpected violence. The victim then suffers fewer traumatic psychological consequences.

SEXUAL HARASSMENT

130 BACKHOUSE, CONSTANCE, and COHEN, LEAH. The Secret Oppression:
Sexual Harassment of Working Women. Toronto: Macmillan of
Canada, 1978, 208 pp.
The Canadian authors of this book had previously specialized in writing about a wide range of issues of concern to
working women. References to sexual harassment were so
numerous that they felt a full-length analysis of the subject was necessary. The result is an integration of dozens

of case histories illustrating that sexual harassment may affect any working woman regardless of age, physical appearance, social status, or job category. "Not surprisingly, we were unable to find a single man who would admit to being a harasser, even men who had been publicly exposed." The authors delve into the history of sexual harassment as an expression of power. Interviews with representatives of personnel departments, management, and unions--no matter how much the subject is glossed over, underemphasized, or interpreted subjectively--point only to the very obvious fact that sexual harassment is very pervasive and exemplifies male domination. The authors also offer short-term action plans to employees, management, and unions as well as long-range societal solutions to a volatile problem. Surprisingly, for such a thorough treatment, the book has no index.

131   ETZCORN, PAMELA. "Dealing with Sexual Harassment" Women's Work 5, no. 5 (September/October 1979):11-14.
      This piece emphasizes not only the economic unfairness of workplace sexual harassment but also the anxieties that result from such constant stress. It lists agencies that serve women in need of assistance.

132   FARLEY, LIN. Sexual Shakedown: The Sexual Harassment of Women on the Job. New York: McGraw-Hill, 1978, 228 pp.
      Lin Farley relentlessly names the abuses and abusers in sexual harassments. It is as difficult for a woman to name sexual harassment as the reason for leaving her job or for being fired as it used to be for women to discuss rape in the courtroom, where they were also disbelieved and humiliated. But due to the efforts of Farley, Catherine MacKinnon (entry 133), and others, the climate is changing. Now talked about more openly, sexual coercion is seen as another way in which women are abused and as an important cause of their continuing second-class economic status. Moreover, it is prevalent on college campuses, where it affects both students and staff, and throughout the world of work. Principal offenders are employers who promote men over women, harbor harassers to protect the company, and thus force women to leave their jobs and forfeit fringe benefits, seniority rights, on-the-job training, and a good employment record. Farley says that unions too have frequently been guilty of sexual harassment. Her proposal that Title VII of the 1964 Civil Rights Act could offer a civil remedy has subsequently been realized in the 1980 Guidelines of the federal Equal Employment Opportunities Commission. Sexual harassment is now defined as sex discrimination.

Sexual Harassment

Farley concludes that "female oppression at work is the result of nearly universal male power to hire and fire. Men control the means of economic survival. This control, however, is also used to coerce women sexually. Institutionalized male power has thus created its own means of maintaining its superior position--by socially enlisting women's cooperation in their own sexual subservience and accomplishing this by rewarding them when they do and punishing them when they do not. Work, the ostensible equalizer, and the means to her economic independence is subsequently transformed into new enslavement."

133 MacKINNON, CATHERINE A. Sexual Harassment of Working Women: A Case of Sex Discrimination. New Haven: Yale University Press, 1979, 312 pp.
    The legal intricacies in this book bear study. To some extent, the author successfully simplifies difficult concepts for interested lay readers. Nevertheless, feminist lawyers undertaking sexual harassment cases will be the principal readers. Extensive chapter notes amplify and elucidate inequality in the workplace. Sexual harassment is yet another long-hidden abuse of women that is now being revealed in all its ugliness. As the author comments in the introduction, "Sexual harassment at work undercuts women's potential for social equality in two interpenetrated ways: by using her employment to coerce her sexually, while using her sexual position to coerce her economically. Legal recognition that sexual harassment is sex discrimination in employment would help women break the bond between material survival and sexual exploitation. It would support and legitimize women's economic equality and sexual self-determination at a point at which the two are linked."

SOCIOLOGICAL INQUIRIES

134 BARNETT, NONA J., and FEILD, HUBERT S. "Sex Differences in University Students' Attitudes Toward Rape." Journal of College Student Personnel 18, no. 2 (March 1967):93-96.
    Surprisingly, male college students still support many of the myths regarding rape and are insensitive to the physiological and psychological trauma of rape for women. The study demonstrates the need for rape education programs for men and women.

Rape

135 CONNELL, NOREEN, and WILSON, CASSANDRA. Rape: The First
     Sourcebook for Women. New York: New American Library,
     1974, 283 pp.
          The book, prepared by the New York Radical Feminists,
     describes, in its totality, the process of consciousness
     raising, speaking out, theory and research, and finally
     political action--a complex experience of growing awareness
     and involvement that led to the formulation of goals to
     eliminate rape. New York Radical Feminists were among the
     first to advocate change in the law; psychological research
     on the characteristics of rapists, victims, and psycholo-
     gists; and reeducation for any person dealing with a rape
     victim. The group also advocated backing of political
     candidates who recognized the need for change; formulating
     of procedures to help victims, including the use of female
     detectives and judges; and improving living conditions and
     transportation in areas where the crime was most prevalent.

136 FEILD, HUBERT S. "Attitudes Toward Rape: A Comparative
     Analysis of Police, Rapists, Crisis Counselors, and
     Citizens." Journal of Personality and Social Psychology,
     36, no. 2 (February 1978):156-79.
          Although attitudes toward rape have been regarded as
     important in rape research, few data have been collected.
     The present investigation is designed to (a) study the
     scope of rape attitudes; (b) explore the relationships
     between perceptions of rape and the background character-
     istics of rapists, police, crisis counselors, and the
     public; and (c) determine how these groups might differ in
     their attitudes toward rape. Data from 1,448 subjects iden-
     tified sex, race, and marital status as the most important
     characteristics for predicting attitudes toward rape.
     There were highly significant differences among the groups
     in the perception of rape. Counselors differed from police,
     the public, and rapists in their views of rape. The public
     and police were most similar. The police and rapists did
     not differ on half of the attitudinal dimensions. Implica-
     tions of the results are discussed in terms of attitude
     toward rapists.

137 GELLES, RICHARD J. "Power, Sex, and Violence: The Case of
     Marital Rape." The Family Coordinator 26, no. 4
     (October 1977):339-47.
          Gelles considers the implications of socializing women
     into believing they are not raped when they are coerced
     into sexual relations with their husband. Since women be-
     lieve that rape must be accompanied by physical force and
     violence, they are unlikely to report verbal coercion and

Rape

Sociological Inquiries

       intimidation to agencies. Only social, attitudinal, and
moral changes will lead to improvement in the law on marital rape. Marital rape is an important area of investigation for social scientists. It exposes the power
relationships and range and nature of sexual activities
in the family.

138   DUKES, RICHARD L., with MATTLEY, CHRISTINE L. "Predicting
      Rape Victim Reportage." Sociology and Social Research 62
      (October 1977):63-84.
          Forty-five recent rape victims were interviewed in an
attempt to explain why some victims report offenses to
police while others do not. Findings disclosed that for
crimes in which victim fear is characteristic, an extremely
frightened victim is likely to report the crime only if
police are perceived as considerate and nonthreatening to
her.

139   HOLMSTROM, LYNDA LYTLE, and BURGESS, ANN WOLBERT. "Rape: The
      Husband's and Boyfriend's Initial Reactions." Family
      Coordinator 28 (July 1979):321-30.
          This survey covered 146 victims of rape. It began with
an open-ended question to determine how husbands, boyfriends,
and the victim react to the rape. The authors attempted to
conceptualize the reactions to the crime among those with
whom the victim was most intimately involved. Husbands and
boyfriends were frequently concerned with their own feelings,
trying to decide whether they had been hurt more than the
victim, wanting to "get the guy," and "if only" reactions.
Men also had to cope with the wife's or girlfriend's psychological crisis by discussing rape as a violent act,
understanding the woman's new phobias, resuming sexual
relations, and coping with the legal process. By precipi-
tating a crisis, a rape dramatically illuminates certain
attitudes and role expectations, which then become more
visible in the routine of everyday life. Husbands' and
boyfriends' reactions indicate assumptions about sexual
access underlying relationships in more normal circumstances.

140   HOROS, CAROL V. Rape. New Canaan, Conn.: Tobey Publishing
      Co., 1974, 140 pp.
          Horos explores numerous aspects of the crime of rape:
characteristics of offender and victim, history of rape
and rape laws, ways to prevent and report the crime,
medical treatment, court procedures and trial, and emotional support for victims. She outlines procedures and
suggests guidelines for establishing and listing rape crisis
centers across the country.

141 KRULEWITZ, JUDITH E., and PAYNE, ELAINE JOHN!
About Rape: Effects of Rapist Force, Obs
Role Attitudes." Journal of Applied Social Psychology o,
no. 4 (October-December 1978):291-305.
This study investigated subjects' perceptions of a
hypothetical rape situation based upon the amount of force
used, the sex of the subjects, and the subjects' attitudes
toward feminism. Subjects expressed greater certainty that
a rape had actually occurred in cases where the assailant
increased reliance upon force. Women with traditional
attitudes believed that the more force used by the assailant, the greater the probability that rape had occurred.
Profeminist women perceived the assault as rape whatever
the force level. This is one of several studies showing
how sex-role stereotyping of women as being respectable or
not, based upon their degree of resistance to an assault,
also influences jury decisions. Women are held responsible
for protecting their own sexual purity.

142 O'SULLIVAN, ELIZABETHANN. "What Has Happened to Rape Crisis
Centers? A Look at Their Structures, Members, and Funding."
Victimology, 3, no. 1-2 (1978-1979):45-62.
This article employs the responses from ninety rape
crisis centers to a mail survey to achieve three objectives:
(1) to fill in a segment of the history of the antirape
movement and the Women's Movement in the United States by
providing material for assessing their impact; (2) to identify organizational trends and provide a better basis for
self-analysis and decision-making by individual rape crisis
centers; and (3) to help guide development of similar organ-
izations, also grassroot, such as shelters for battered
women.

143 RUSSELL, DIANA. The Politics of Rape: The Victim's Perspective. New York: Stein and Day, 1975, 311 pp. Bibliog.
Like Brownmiller's Against Our Will, written in the same
year, this book is already a modern feminist classic.
Russell looks at rape through a series of interviews with
twenty-two rape victims, rebutting popular myths. She also
devotes a large part of her book to rape within marriage,
even though it has not, until recently, been generally
recognized as a crime. Like Brownmiller, she sees rape as
the result of the different socialization of males and
females.

144 SCHWENDINGER, J., and SCHWENDINGER, H. "Rape Myths: In Legal,
Theoretical and Everyday Practice." Crime and Social
Justice: Journal of Radical Criminology 1 (1974):18-26.

iological Inquiries

This article debunks rape myths with vivid examples written from a socialist point of view. Crimes of violence are produced by capitalism, which will continue to foster the hatred and contempt of certain men toward women. The Women's Movement can prevent rape only by political struggle to eliminate bourgeois domination of everyday life, which occurs through the sexual double standard that typifies this society.

145 SHOTLAND, R. L., and STRAW, M. K. "Bystander Response to an Assault When a Man Attacks a Woman." Journal of Personality and Social Psychology 34, no. 5 (1976):990-99.
The authors describe, in statistical terms, a series of psychodramas, whereby a street quarrel is set up and a woman attacked, while bystanders (the subjects of the experiment) stand around passively. According to subjects' responses, women who were strangers to attackers were perceived as needing more help than married women (who presumably should know how to defend themselves from brutality). The authors discuss the implications for social control.

146 VINSEL, ANNE. "Rape: A Review Essay." Personality and Social Psychology Bulletin 3, no. 2 (Spring 1977):183-89.
This review essay of Brownmiller's Against Our Will and Russell's The Politics of Rape initiates a consideration of social psychology's failure thus far to address the causes and consequences of rape in this society. Vinsel says that investigations of victims' reactions, although important, seem to have been conducted at the expense of thinking about the roots of rape as a social phenomenon. She thinks that the two books, although outside social psychology per se, may provide a starting point for a social-psychological investigation of rape.

THEORETICAL PERSPECTIVES

147 BURT, MARTHA R. "Cultural Myths and Supports for Rape." Journal of Personality and Social Psychology 38, no. 2 (February 1980):217-30.
The author says her research shows that many Americans believe many rape myths; these beliefs are strongly connected to other deeply-held attitudes, such as sex-role stereotyping, distrust of the opposite sex, and acceptance of interpersonal violence. She suggests combatting sex-role stereotyping at a very early age, before attitudes

begin to affect behavior. As a result of the combined pressures of sex-role stereotyping and the psychological availability of violence, the United States has the highest rape rate of any industrialized country. As it is now, preventing rape is tantamount to revamping a significant number of our societal values. An accurate theoretical understanding of assaultive behavior and attitudes toward rape will help make efforts at social change more effective.

148 GRIFFIN, SUSAN. "Rape: The All-American Crime." Ramparts 10 (September 1971):26-35.

Griffin shows the rape myths for what they are: A male-dominated society needs an underpinning for the status-quo. Men define "chastity." Women who do not conform to the standards are, according to Griffin, candidates for rape. Thus, women are kept in their place. More important, the laws governing rape protect the rights of men as possessors of women and reinforce the idea that rape is a crime committed by men against men, rather than against women. This is one of the first exposés of rape as an instrument of power.

149 _____. Rape: The Power of Consciousness. New York: Harper & Row, 1979, 134 pp. Appendix: List of Rape Crisis Centers.

This sequel to "Rape: The All American Crime" (entry 148), published eight years later, sees women's new ability to imagine a world without rape and other forms of patriarchal violence as a direct result of naming the oppression. In the course of these essays, Griffin explains her rejection of the student Left, of which she had been a member, because it regarded rape, and ultimately women, as negligible in the order of things. The process of women healing women through rape centers and the existence of a women's health network (based on the assumption that women's bodies ought to be cared for) challenged the belief that women ought to suffer and also figures prominently in their new consciousness. Griffin, along with Mary Daly and Adrienne Rich, is one of the most inspirational poet-politicians. The book's last chapter is a collage: Words from the Women's Movement and sexist observations from both ancient and modern times should resonate with the reader's own experiences. The appendix lists rape crisis centers state-by-state and the address of the National Coalition Against Sexual Assault, for those seeking current information.

150 HARTWIG, PATRICIA A., and SANDUR, GEORGETTE BENNETT. "Rape Victims: Reasons, Responses, Reforms." Intellect 103, no. 2366 (May-June 1975):507-11.

Rape

Theoretical Perspectives

> This article discusses the social and legal aspects of
rape in a cultural context. In regard to the development
of sex-role stereotypes, the authors maintain that shifting
the blame onto the victim subconsciously served as a self-
protective mechanism for men and women. Today, two major
problems of rape research are the lack of standarized definitions of the crime from state to state and the absence of
valid, reliable statistics on rape. For example, words
like "force" and "consent" vary in meaning and include in
their definitions acts formerly excluded.

151   LINDSEY, KAREN et al. "Aspects of Rape." The Second Wave:
      A Magazine of the New Feminism 2, no. 2 (1972):28-29.
      The authors discuss rape from a feminist perspective as
a tool for keeping women in the place created for them by
male-dominated society. In rape, the assailant symbolically
violates both another man's property and the victim's body.
The psychological trauma, pain, and humiliation of the victim are ignored. Her worth as property is devalued. Rape
will continue until the present system of sex-role socialization and sexual myths is changed.

152   SHORTER, EDWARD. "On Writing the History of Rape." Signs 3,
      no. 2 (Winter 1977):471-82.
      Shorter, a historian, claims that Brownmiller's Against
Our Will is an inadequate history of rape, that it is full
of gaps. He denies her assertion that rape has always rep-
resented power-politics in a male-dominated society. He
suggests that the politicizing of rape is a new development
from the 1960s, which can be understood only by examining
the frequency of rape from one epoch to another, systemati-
cally reviewing differences in forcible sex from group to
group, and differentiating "with concrete evidence the
extent to which 'normal' sexual encounters resemble rape."

Chapter 4
Sexual Abuse of Children

The medical profession and other agencies confronted with long-standing evidence of child abuse first began to deal seriously with the problem after Dr. Henry Kempe and his colleagues defined its unmistakable symptoms in the early 1970s. (Charles Henry Kempe and Ray E. Helfer, eds. Helping the Battered Child and His Family [Philadelphia: Lippincott, 1972]).

Although every state had some legislation against child abuse before the 1970s, most laws were ineffective in preventing abuse, apprehending abusers, or treating victims. One of the chief reasons for not being able to attack the problem of child abuse effectively earlier was the widespread unwillingness of doctors and others who were aware of it to report cases.

The Federal Child Abuse and Treatment Act of 1974 provided clout for the drive to establish effective programs. It also prescribed severe penalties for exploiting children through pornographic entertainment (the infamous "chicken porn" industry), which became a felony. The fourth resolution passed at the National Women's Conference held in Houston in 1978 urged continued funding and support for the prevention of abuse and the treatment of abused children and their parents. The plank included sexual abuse, which the law defined as the obscene or pornographic photographing, filming, or depiction of children for commercial purposes, or rape, molestation, incest, prostitution, and other forms of sexual exploitation, which harm or threaten the child's health or welfare.

In Sexually Victimized Children (entry 158), David Finkelhor notes that child abuse is a public issue of long standing. It was taken up both by the earlier child protection lobby, which resulted in federal legislation, and later, as the resolution passed at the Conference held in Houston shows, by the Women's Movement, which regards sexual abuse as a subcategory of rape. Without question, incest is a form of child abuse. Child abuse generally signifies beating and other forms of physical mistreatment, including neglect, over a long period, with probable psychological damage as well.

Incest is unique in that the perpetrator's intent at the onset is rarely to inflict harm. Incest may sometimes be an extension of an originally loving parent/child relationship that at some point exceeds appropriate boundaries. It shares with child abuse the inflicting of psychological damage of possible lifelong duration. As in other forms of child abuse, the incestuous relationship extends over a period of some months and, most frequently, years.

The perpetrator is most often a beloved father, whose betrayal of the child's trust through sexual victimization makes the crime more heinous and less forgiveable. How the child reacts to sexual victimization is determined also by age and maturity, whether or not force is used, and the degree of shame or guilt evoked by participation. More important, perhaps, is the reaction of the mother and of adult professionals who become involved in the case.

Many women who were incest victims carry the burden of unwarranted guilt for years. Only recently have they begun to articulate their feelings. Until recently, the incest victim was treated in court just as the rape victim had been routinely treated, that is, exposed to all the indignities of being exhibited publicly before a disbelieving audience.

All civilizations and cultures have issued edicts against incest. Some have nevertheless allowed its practice by royalty and by certain other privileged classes. For example, Cleopatra was a notable product of such an intrafamily union. Today, we are witnessing a trend toward the softening of penalties against incest in some quarters. In "The Disappearance of the Incest Taboo" (entry 155), Yehudi Cohen writes that a few years ago in Sweden, in the wake of a marriage between brother and sister, who had been raised totally apart by different foster parents and who had had several children, an official Swedish Judicial Committee examined the question and proposed the removal of criminal sanctions. The question, Cohen writes, will eventually be decided by the Swedish Parliament. That case and such events as the showing of a sympathetic film about mother/son incest ("Luna") in theaters throughout the United States in 1980 may signal that incest prohibitions will carry fewer penalties in years to come. Nevertheless, bitter struggles will ensue between the pro- and anti-incest factions before such a state of affairs becomes acceptable.

A conference entitled "Sexual Victimization of Children: Trauma, Trial, and Treatment," sponsored by the Child Sexual Abuse Victim Assistance Project of Children's Hospital National Medical Center in Washington, D.C., was held in New York in 1979. As reported in the New York Times (3 December 1979), Professor LeRoy Schultz of West Virginia State University's School of Social Work told the audience of about 300 people that there are approximately 5,000 cases of incest and between 200,000 and 500,000 cases of sexual molestation of children per year nationally. Reported cases are thought to represent only a small percentage of the actual incidence. Schultz caused a furor by suggesting that recent and still unpublished evidence will show that some incestuous experiences "may be either a positive, healing experience or at worst, neutral and dull." The conferees overwhelmingly repudiated Schultz's claim. Conference speakers agreed, however, that any approach to incest is hampered by a notable lack of reliable data and of people professionally trained to deal with the subject's many facets.

Treatment programs do utilize family and group therapy to help other members of the family function in a healthier way. As more people have sought help, greater attention has been given to treatment and to the legal and protective issues. The following entries reflect these considerations. Consistent with the theme of the bibliography, violence against women, the articles treat only father/daughter (male adult/girl child) incestuous relationships and their damaging effects.

PERSONAL ACCOUNTS

153   ARMSTRONG, LOUISE. <u>Kiss Daddy Goodnight: A Speak-out on
      Incest</u>. New York: Hawthorne, 1978, 256 pp. Bibliog.
         The author agrees with other writers that talking about,
      not practicing, incest is taboo. Armstrong questions why
      it is so important for the family where incest is occurring
      to remain intact--a point upon which many therapists insist--
      while divorce occurs regularly when a woman does something
      her husband finds offensive, such as aging. There is no
      elaborate social machinery to forestall a family breakup.
      Despite the rather satirical tone of this angry feminist's
      book, it is a solid work asking many hard, unanswered ques-
      tions. Since men are permitted, implicitly and explicitly,
      to exploit others in order to satisfy their sexual needs,
      why is there surprise when men extend the permission to in-
      clude their own children? Society is as much in collusion
      as mothers with fathers' sexual abuse. Sexual abuse de-
      pends upon furtiveness. If the boundaries to legitimate
      sexual activity were clearly demarcated, exploitation would
      not occur. This book's outspoken accounts of hitherto
      secret experiences, which Armstrong obtained by placing
      notices in a number of feminist publications and through
      referrals from friends, are the kind of frank exposure that
      may help eradicate this kind of sexual abuse. Openness,
      not collusion, is the answer. Added features of this book,
      written for a general audience, are a bibliography and a
      list of facilities with treatment programs for incest
      victims.

154   BRADY, KATHERINE. <u>Father's Days: A True Story of Incest</u>.
      New York: Seaview Books, 1979, 216 pp.
         Brady recounts father-daughter incest over a decade with
      a vivid picture of the incubus under which she lived. This
      is a particularly pathetic, credible story, which should
      make clear the stresses of such a life: Brady's deep need
      to maintain the facade of happy family cohesiveness as a
      supposedly model high school student, while struggling with
      shame and deep depression in an unwanted relationship; un-
      successful marriage and divorce; unsatisfactory lesbian
      relationships; and eventually more successful therapy lead-
      ing to a breakthrough to understanding, freedom, and re-
      union with her two daughters, who had been removed from her
      care by court order. Brady's reliving of a tortured child-
      hood and youth without supportive help of any kind is an
      authentic portrayal of countless themes that research stud-
      ies are now revealing.

THEORETICAL CONCEPTS

155   COHEN, YEHUDI. "The Disappearance of the Incest Taboo."
       Human Nature 1, no. 7 (1978):72-78.
           An anthropologist, Cohen states that the traditional
       reasons for avoiding marriage with one's near relatives
       are no longer relevant. He attributes the origin of the
       taboo to the necessity of establishing alliances with dis-
       tant trading partners. But once institutions designed to
       organize official trade networks were established, the rea-
       sons for invoking the taboo were reduced. Nor do genetic
       defects occur frequently enough to justify the prohibition.
       Cohen suggests that genetic inbreeding may aid the process
       of "genetic cleansing and a reduction of detrimental re-
       cessive genes and an increase in beneficial recessive
       genes." On the other hand, social, emotional, and psycho-
       logical well-being in a diversified society depends upon
       access to a wide variety of ideas, viewpoints, life-styles,
       and social relations. These are valid reasons for marrying
       outside the family. Today incestuous relationships are
       maintained only by individuals who are isolated from the
       cultural mainstream. Cohen agrees that today incest taboos
       limit intense family relationships and assure the detach-
       ment that emotional maturity requires. He suggests that,
       as in homosexual relationships, incestuous relationships
       between consenting adults may someday be regarded as the
       partners' concern alone.

156   De MOTT, BENJAMIN. "Up Front/The Pro-Incest Lobby."
       Psychology Today 13, no. 10 (March 1980):11-18.
           De Mott's comments on allegedly "positive" incest experi-
       ences, increasingly being discussed in some quarters today,
       are highly critical of the proponents' claim to responsible
       scholarship and of their background experiences. Yet there
       is evidence that the proincest lobby is growing stronger:
       (1) In 1978, a paper before the American Psychiatric Asso-
       ciation's Institute on Hospital and Community Psychiatry
       revealed the psychologist-author's own positive, even bene-
       ficial, experiences of incest; (2) A report by the Sex
       Information and Education Council of the United States
       (SIECUS) urged fresh research on incest and advocated more
       relaxed family sexual relationships to help end adolescent
       promiscuity outside the family with its epidemic of unwanted
       pregnancies; (3) There is in preparation a book with the
       working title The Last Taboo: The Other Side of Incest, by
       Warren Farrell who, according to De Mott is "without repu-
       tation as a sexology researcher." (4) Incest was mentioned

Theoretical Concepts

four times over a six-month period in Ann Landers' influen-
tial advice column; (5) Two recent films dealing with incest
(Flesh and Blood and Luna) have been shown on television
and in many theaters. For easing the taboo, lobbyists propose arguments that may appeal to many in our "open" society:
that the incidence of incest is so high (more than 40,000
cases a year) that prohibition is absurd; that guilt causes
more harm than the act itself; and that incestuous acts are
less destructive than parents' seductive behavior, short of
incest. Although the "decriminalizers" emphasize that
child abuse can and should be separated from "consensual
incest," none seems to consider that the elder partner also
can dupe the younger into perceiving exploitive advances as
love.

157   FINKELHOR, DAVID. "Psychological, Cultural and Family Factors
      in Incest and Family Sexual Abuse." Journal of Marriage
      and Family Counseling 4, no. 4 (October 1978):41-49.
         Finkelhor, a social psychologist, notes that incestuous
      individuals are authoritarian, passive, and alcoholic. Yet,
      there must be many more people with such characteristics than
      there are people who in fact practice incest. What other
      ingredients go into the character makeup of incest offenders?
      Finkelhor says that clinical findings consistently show that
      incest occurs after a breakdown of sexual relations between
      husband and wife. The mother appears to be particularly
      withdrawn, depressed, and incapacitated. The mother-daughter
      relationship also deteriorates. Daughters take over sexual
      functions and other responsibilities from mothers. This
      kind of "deal" serves the mother's own purposes. Incestuous
      relations arise also in a milieu of deprivation and isola-
      tion, in a family that has little concept of appropriate
      sexual boundaries, combined with such opportunity factors
      as the mother's absence from home. In addition, community
      attitudes and family history play a part.

158   _____. Sexually Victimized Children. New York: The Free
      Press, 1979, 228 pp. Bibliog.
         Finkelhor acknowledges at the outset the importance of
      the political context for the prominence given new social
      problems. In the case of sexual abuse of children, an
      alliance between two experienced political constituencies
      championed the cause: the Child Protection Lobby, composed
      of physicians and social workers; and the Women's Movement,
      which in the last decade brought rape and wife battery to
      public attention. Each group has tried to assimilate the
      problem into the framework of old problems around which it
      had successfully campaigned, the physical abuse of children

for the former and rape for the latter. Finkelhor asserts
that while the sexual assault of children has similarities
and differences to both, it is, in fact, unique. Of the
many different terms he might have chosen (sexual abuse,
child molestation, sexual victimization, sexual harassment,
sexual assault, child rape, sexual misuse--each emphasizing
a slightly different aspect of the phenomenon), he favored
"sexual victimization," which emphasizes that the child is
victimized by reason of its age, naïveté, and relationship
to the older person rather than by the aggressive intent of
the abuser. He recognizes that the term "sexual victimization" has a pejorative connotation and political and moral
implications as well, yet feels that it is still useful
within a scientific investigation. The study is intended
to encourage renewed social and legal concern with the
problem.

159   GOODWIN, JEAN et al. "Incest Hoax: False Accusations, False
      Denials." Bulletin of the American Academy of Psychiatry
      and Law 6, no. 3 (1978):269-76.
          Although reported accusations of incest are rarely false,
      legal and mental health professionals tend to suspect them.
      Freud's belief that reports of patients' incest were pure
      fantasy continues to influence professionals. The authors
      emphasize the importance of expertise in investigating
      accusations, because the law requires reporting sexual
      abuse of children. "Persistent and methodical investiga-
      tion tends to yield a consensually credible view of what
      really happened. In order to make a diagnosis of incest
      hoax, the investigator must thoroughly understand the
      mechanics of the hoax and the psychodynamics of the per-
      petrator." Failure to recognize a false denial also can
      delay treatment of the perpetrator, subject the family to
      unnecessary legal action, and encourage the future use of
      similar manipulative techniques. Similarly, failure to
      recognize a false retraction may leave the victim in danger
      of further sexual abuse or physical punishment. The authors
      present guidelines to help verify an accusation of incest.

160   HERMAN, JUDITH, and HIRSCHMAN, LISA. "Father-Daughter Incest."
      Signs 2, no. 4 (Summer 1977):735-56.
          Feminists Herman and Hirschman offer a number of original,
      important points to account for the origin of the incest
      taboo, which they trace back to earliest times. The authors
      recognize it as the first, basic peace treaty between power-
      ful men over their possessions: women. The treaty was
      created and enforced by men, who can also violate it. Pa-
      triarchal society abhors incest between mother and son,

which is an affront to the father's prerogatives. Father-
daughter incest carries considerably less weight and therefore is more frequent. As many surveys show, incest
offenders are frequently family tyrants. "The greater the
degree of male supremacy in any culture, the greater the
likelihood of father-daughter incest." The authors also
speculate on why women observe the taboo so scrupulously.
They suggest that because women have historically been both
the sexual property of their husbands and those with primary
responsibility for the children, they understand the harmful
effects of engaging in incest where there is a vast inequality of power. The authors find that therapy for victims is
an insufficient response to the problem of incest. More
effective is public revelation. Consciousness-raising contributes far more to women's liberation. In practical terms,
prevention rather than treatment is indicated. Important
also are support of the mother's role in the family and the
strengthening of protective services for women and children,
including adequate financial support, free round-the-clock
child care, refuge facilities for women in crisis, and
rigorous enforcement of the law by women law officers.
Father-daughter incest will end only when male supremacy
ends.

161   MEISELMAN, KARIN. Incest: A Psychological Study of Causes
      and Effects with Treatment Recommendations. San Francisco:
      Jossey-Bass, 1979, 366 pp. Bibliog.
          Meiselman acknowledges in her preface that she has inte-
      grated previous literature on the psychology of incest with
      her own findings. Chapter 1 summarizes anthropological and
      sociological views on the origin and maintenance of the
      incest taboo. Chapter 2 discusses the advantages and in-
      herent problems of various strategies for researching incest
      behavior. Chapter 3 delineates the data collection methods
      employed in the present study and describes briefly, the
      psychotherapeutic sample of incest cases and of the control
      group of clinic patients with no history of incest. The
      remainder of the book emphasizes the psychological causes
      and long-term effects of overt incest between father and
      daughter, mother and son, and siblings.

162   ROSENFELD, ALVIN A. "Endogamic Incest and the Victim-
      Perpetrator Model." American Journal of Diseases of
      Children 133, no. 4 (April 1979):406-10.
          Rosenfeld suggests that mandatory reporting of incest to
      the judicial system often deprives even the most experienced
      therapists of discretion and gives responsibility to indi-
      viduals with fewer skills. If the law is not automatically

involved, the therapist has the responsibility of determining the acceptability of the child's surroundings. Rosenfeld characterizes the endogamic (inbreeding) family as having traits of pathological concealment and as agreeing implicitly to maintain the appearance of a normal intact family. The parents are immature, whether the father behaves generally in a domineering or submissive way; the mother is insecure; and the child is needy and deprived. It is ironic that the molesting parent is often the more nurturing one, loved and trusted by the victim. His sexual activities may also conform to the child's psychosexual development, being pleasurable but secretive. Although the child may have learned seductive behavior, she does not necessarily recognize its sexual meaning in an adult way. This renders her more easily exploitable. The courtroom's adversarial conditions exacerbate the damage, for the child now becomes "an emotional orphan," without anyone to turn to, besides being blamed for the situation. Family dissolution is difficult financially because the molestor is also the breadwinner. Foster care may also involve incest, because the child has learned the technique for getting affection. Finally, family dissolution also has serious consequences for uninvolved siblings who have shared the same home and emotional climate. Rosenfeld concludes that therapeutic interventions must be tailored to the individual family's style and needs, but may require legal backup or the threat of dissolution.

163   RESENFELD, ALVIN A. et al. "Fantasy and Reality in Patients' Reports of Incest. Journal of Clinical Psychiatry 40, no. 4 (April 1979):159-64.
      Rosenfeld and colleagues discuss some of the difficulties clinicians face trying to assess patients' reports of incest. Confusion arises over psychosexual development, repression of a traumatic experience, and the child's phase of cognitive development. The person who is free from major psychiatric illness usually reports clearly and accurately about molestation that occurred after the age of nine years. A clinician, in reviewing eight clinical questions, will be able to determine whether a reported case of incest is authentic, and thus whether legal procedures are justified.

164   SUMMIT, ROLAND, and KRYSO, ANN. "Sexual Abuse of Children: A Clinical Spectrum." American Journal of Orthopsychiatry 48, no. 2 (April 1978):237-51.
      This study examines a wide range of sexual involvement, from variations on normal behavior to that which is clearly criminal. The authors maintain that the most concealed form of child abuse deserves to be addressed with the same degree

of enlightenment and with helping resources similar to those that have revolutionized the approach to other forms of abuse. They identify ten types of child sexual molestation: (1) incidental sexual contact; (2) ideological sexual contact, that is, a search for ways to express modern social values that, however, stimulate more sexual curiosity than the child is prepared to accept. This newest form of molestation presents a dilemma when it involves explicit sexual behavior without clear intent to harm. (3) psychotic intrusion, probably the least frequent type; (4) incest in a rustic environment outside the dominant cultural mores; (5) true endogamous incest with various levels of betrayal. From this type, a bizarre spin-off endows the victim with attributes of dangerous attractiveness, such as those found in witchcraft, and deprives her of any respect. (6) misogynous incest, with the daughter viewed as the possession of a woman-hating father; (7) imperious incest by a devout fundamentalist spouting Christian doctrine and quoting the Scriptures to justify the daughter's role; (8) pedophilic incest, which has for the child a redeeming feature in that she is relatively free from stigma or guilt; (9) incest where the rapist confuses masculinity with power and uses the child victim's fear to feel sexually adequate; (10) perverse incest, which relies upon pornography and kinky sex, with multiple partners for ritual pleasure. This is very similar to the ideological category described above.

TREATMENT CONSIDERATIONS

165 ANDERSON, DEBORAH, and TEN BENSEL, ROBERT W. "Counseling the Family in Which Incest Has Occurred." Medical Aspects of Human Sexuality 13, no. 4 (April 1979):143-44.

Described as a "Brief Guide to Office Counseling," this straightforward, no-nonsense outline describes symptoms and lists measures a physician should take in cases where he or she suspects incest. It discusses the interview and physical examination, initial crisis situation, and reporting of the incest. The authors caution that effective counseling demands alertness to signs of deviant sexual behavior within a family and the ability to deal with the crisis situation, including knowledge of how community services function and the realization that physicians are only a part of a network of services a community can provide. But the physician is in a key position to provide support to the child and her family by explaining what available services might be

appropriate and continuing to work together with other personnel as the family progresses in treatment. Early detec-
tion is necessary to protect children from further incest
and also to help make families more functional.

166   BURGESS, ANN WOLBERT; GROTH, A. NICHOLAS; HOLMSTROM, LYNDA
      LYTLE; and SGROI, SUZANNE M. Sexual Assault of Children
      and Adolescents. Lexington, Mass.: Lexington Books,
      1978, 245 pp. Bibliog. and references.
         This is a textbook of readings on treatment and manage-
      ment of sexual offenders, victims, and their families. A
      team of well-known therapists look at psychological mal-
      function from a variety of perspectives and offer help to
      the health professional dealing with the problem. Sgroi,
      affiliated with a treatment center in Hartford, Connecticut,
      deplores widespread institutional failure to grapple with
      the difficult problem of child sexual abuse at each level,
      beginning with general reluctance to report probable cases
      to the proper agencies that can deal with the abuser and,
      generally, his wife as accessory; the reluctance of the
      judicial system to initiate the necessary action; and the
      equivocation of the medical profession about performing
      necessary physical examinations of children who have been
      sexually abused. Her overview sets the tone for succeeding
      papers by specialists who feel that a lack of treatment
      methodology has led to chaotic conditions and hampers any
      real advances in the cure of offenders and victims. There
      is a consensus that sexual abuse has certain common themes:
      retaliation by the husband against the wife for actual or
      imagined unfaithfulness; a sense of entitlement to one's
      children as personal property; loneliness and a need for
      intimacy and close affiliation with another person; and
      social isolation and depression. Involvement of the crim-
      inal justice system provides a powerful authoritarian in-
      centive for changing behavior and stopping sexual abuse.

167   BUTLER, SANDRA. Conspiracy of Silence: The Trauma of Incest.
      San Francisco: New Glide Publications, 1978, 208 pp.
      Bibliog.
         Sandra Butler adds an important element to the growing
      literature on incest and child molestation. While noting
      the underlying psychopathology of an incestuous family, she
      attributes equal importance to the socialization of men and
      women. "Coupled with the self-perpetuating nature of most
      forms of abuse is the problem of the rigidly patriarchal
      values and world view held by so many sexual aggressors,
      which is expressed in their attitudes and relationships
      within their homes and outside of them." Powerless in the

Treatment Considerations

outside world but socialized to believe that power is a
male's natural right, men who become aggressors are des-
potic and tyrannical at home. Having grown up most usually
in chaotic environments, such men have no appropriate model
and find no means for satisfying unfulfilled needs for power
and love except through preying on their children. Butler
is less condemnatory than other writers of the wives who
are usually·blamed as tacit partners in incestuous homes:
"Women who cannot meet traditional responsibilities because
they are suffering emotionally or physically . . . are made
to carry the burden of guilt for the emotional disruption
that may result from their abdication." As to the victims,
the children in an eroding family at an early age sense
what is required to keep the family together and will com-
ply even at the price of their own victimization. She di-
rects her severest criticisms at the "professional family"--
staff of schools, churches, health and social agencies, the
police and courts--all of whom consistently fail to acknowl-
edge the taboo subject, claim ignorance of its manifestations, fail to offer supportive services or to deal
adequately with human need in its rawest form, or handle
it so judgmentally and harshly that recovery appears un-
likely. She calls on all helping agencies to create a
supportive environment in which constructive actions may
be taken.

168   COURTOIS, CHRISTINE A. "Victims of Rape and Incest."
      Counseling Psychologist 8, no. 1 (1979):38-40.
      The author presents principles on the counseling and
therapy of rape and incest victims and reviews the available data. Mental health professionals can provide victims
with psychological treatment that may be especially critical
to their recovery, since counselors often see victims when
they are in a crisis and most vulnerable. This may be soon
after the assault or when the assault is in the distant
past, but its effects provoke a crisis-like reaction in the
victim. Research on victim response patterns and therapeutic strategies has resulted in the articulation of helpful principles for counselors. Support, acceptance, and
understanding of the victim are especially crucial, since
sexual assault and societal attitudes often result in victims feeling guilty, ashamed, isolated, different, and
soiled. Courtois concludes that both the problems that a
victim faces and the decisions she must make after sexual
assault will require the counselor's assistance in develop-
ing coping skills.

169   DAUGHERTY, MARY KATHERINE. "The Crime of Incest Against the
      Minor Child and the States' Statutory Responses." Journal
      of Family Law 17, no. 1 (1979):93–115.
          Daugherty feels that although a few states have good
      incest laws (Michigan, Ohio, New Hampshire), most states
      need to examine and restructure their laws in order to
      distinguish between the goal of protecting the genetic
      pool and protecting the child from psychological crippling
      for life. As a result of out-of-date incest laws that fail
      to address the issue constructively, there has been an in-
      crease in the number of adolescent runaways and a high in-
      cidence of mental illness, alcoholism, drug abuse, and
      prostitution among female adolescents who have been sex-
      ually abused at home. Courts, too, typically place on
      incest victims the kind of blame that was inflicted (until
      the Women's Movement intervened) on rape victims when, in
      hostile courtroom settings, courts blamed the victim rather
      than the offender.

170   FORWARD, SUSAN, and BUCK, CRAIG. Betrayal of Innocence:
      Incest and Its Devastation. Los Angeles: J. B. Tarcher,
      1978, 198 pp. Bibliog.
          Forward treats incest in terms of aggressors, "silent
      partners" (wives), and the family as a whole. Through a
      combination of methods including those of humanistic psy-
      chology, which emphasizes the development of self-awareness
      and self-esteem, she encourages each individual to take
      charge of his/her life, a particularly appropriate objec-
      tive for treating those involved in incest. As a victim
      who recovered from deep traumatic effects through sympa-
      thetic treatment, she has a special understanding of the
      severe psychological disturbance that is both cause and
      effect. That self-awareness, together with her training
      in intensive group therapy methods and as teacher of other
      mental health professionals, has led her to specialize in
      the treatment of incest. By 1978, she had treated several
      hundred patients. Like other specialists, she identifies
      the underlying causes as family dysfunction, social isola-
      tion, the aggressor's need to reduce his sense of inade-
      quacy, and a strong craving for love or belonging on the
      victim's part. Most incest pairings are father/daughter,
      but Forward also discusses other incestuous relationships.
      Like other specialists treating this now-acknowledged wide-
      spread abuse, she places full responsibility for its initia-
      tion on the aggressor. She cautions, however, that severe
      punishment will effect no cure nor substitute for psycho-
      logical and/or medical treatment. Handling of prosecution
      in the courtroom at the time of the book's appearance (1978)

Treatment Considerations

resembled the routine treatment of rape victims until the
Women's Movement brought improvements; that is, disbelief
and humiliation of the victim and the additional misery in
the case of incest of sending a father to prison, all add-
ing trauma to trauma.

171   GEISER, ROBERT L. Hidden Victims: The Sexual Abuse of
       Children. Boston: Beacon Press, 1979, 191 pp. Bibliog.
       The sexual abuse of children assumes many forms, from
       acts so subtle as to defy detection to vicious acts of
       undisguised hatred. An adult is always responsible for
       abuse, no matter how much the child is brainwashed into
       feeling guilt about being the cause of the molestation.
       The author suggests an end to the sexual abuse of children
       through a national reporting system; broad public education
       programs to promote public awareness; no-nonsense sex educa-
       tion programs in the public schools; research into family
       dysfunction and general programs to strengthen families;
       and the creation of a young adult domestic Peace Corps of
       all youths not in school and consisting of one to two years
       of paid service for work in social welfare agencies. A
       final suggestion, which the author calls utopian, is the
       creation of a Quality of Life Council in 1987 to celebrate
       the anniversary of the signing of the Constitution and to
       assess and evaluate the quality of life in this country two
       hundred years later.

172   GENTRY, CHARLES E. "Incestuous Abuse of Children: The Need
       for an Objective View." Child Welfare 57, no. 6 (1978):
       355-64.
       The author calls for a more objective and less punitive
       approach to incest. He cites some of society's present
       responses: denial, repugnance, guilt by association, anger,
       and uneasy fascination. Through a firm but not severe in-
       tervention, Gentry sees less psychological damage to the
       family and dollar loss to the community. He recommends
       simultaneously minimizing the emotional trauma of all in-
       volved and making family life more functional. Desirable
       measures are counseling, day care provisions, and setting
       of consistent limits. The offender responds better to
       learning acceptable patterns of interaction and communica-
       tion than to incarceration. The caring parent in incestu-
       ous relations is a strength that should be capitalized on
       constructively, with patience and tolerance for dealing
       with depression and self-destructive behavior, because
       intervention may trigger truancy in the children and act-
       ing out by other siblings.

173   GIARRETTO, HENRY. "Humanistic Treatment of Father-Daughter
      Incest." <u>Journal of Humanistic Psychology</u> 18, no. 4
      (Fall 1978):59-76.
           Henry Giarretto's Child Sexual Abuse Treatment Program
      in San Jose, California is acclaimed in many articles about
      incest and viewed as a nearly totally effective model in
      the cure of dysfunctional families. Giarretto describes
      the methods used, which are based upon the belief that
      humanistic psychology has direct applicability to every
      social issue. He wonders whether the same principles and
      methods would also apply to seriously troubled people and
      emphasizes the importance of "self-work," the techniques
      of building up a sense of self-awareness and rejecting any
      rationalizations. Fathers must always admit their respon-
      sibility for initiating the incestuous relationship. Mothers
      must eventually admit their contribution to the underlying
      causes. Even daughters must eventually confront the fact
      they are not entirely helpless victims, and they are en-
      couraged to explore this revelation. Giarretto uses the
      authority of the criminal justice system so that the of-
      fender knows unequivocally that his conduct will not be
      condoned in any way, under any circumstances. He says that
      about ten percent of the participants elude the program's
      efforts and that offenders who participate in order to
      avoid jail must be shown that there are more substantial
      benefits.

174   JUSTICE, BLAIR, and JUSTICE, RITA. <u>The Broken Taboo: Sex in
      the Family</u>. New York: Human Sciences Press, 1979, 304 pp.
      Bibliog.
           This book grew out of a survey the authors made of 112
      families in which incest had occurred. The authors con-
      ducted intensive group therapy with a number of the fam-
      ilies involved, including the children. They also provide
      a comprehensive literature review of studies on incest and
      discuss many other investigators' findings. They contribute
      a significant new element to the rapidly growing literature
      on sexual abuse of children in their classification of per-
      sonality types of fathers who engage in incest. Symbiotic
      personalities who do not know how to meet their emotional
      needs in a nonsexual way, they are introverts, rational-
      izers, or tyrants, each type displaying distinctive sorts
      of behavior. None of them understands how he is trying to
      fulfill deep needs for warmth and affection through inap-
      propriate sex. It appears that all types of incestuous
      fathers can be found on all economic and educational levels.
      The authors concur with other writers that regardless of
      how inviting the daughter's behavior may be, or how deep

Treatment Considerations

her need for affection, the father bears the responsibility for incestuous relations. They recommend consistently taking the kind of legal action, criminal or civil, which best promotes the welfare of the child and her family. The authors favor action brought under child abuse laws (civil law) rather than under incest laws (criminal laws). It is critical that one do something about the victimization of the child rather than punish parents. On the public level, the authors recommend that federal, state, and local welfare agencies, human resources departments, and schools should conduct widespread public information campaigns, just as they have done with child abuse and as the Women's Movement is doing on the issues of rape and battering. They do caution against punitive treatment of the sort advocated by those at the other end of the social spectrum who want no "pampering" of offenders. There is a comprehensive bibliography of both older and current journals and books.

175 MULDOON, LINDA, ed. <u>Incest: Confronting the Silent Crime</u>. St. Paul, Minn.: Program for Victims of Sexual Assault, 1979, 100 pp.

This manual presents data collected between 1970 and 1974 in Ramsey County, Minnesota. It draws upon the experiences of people from many different disciplines participating in the program and is made possible through the use of interagency team process. The process is meant to broaden and deepen each professional's perspective and leads to greater knowledge about, and more effective services for, abused children and their families. Sexual activity between children and a parent or guardian is a destructive reality that requires professional intervention. Mandatory report laws reflect this philosophy. In fact, since the passage of such a law in Minnesota, there has been a marked increase in identified and reported cases. The book assumes that sexual abuse is invariably damaging psychologically; that without intervention abuse will continue and involve others; that a victim's understanding of sexuality is usually distorted and she lacks the verbal skills to express her experience or feelings and is thus hindered in seeking help; that a child reporting abuse should be assumed to be telling the truth unless there is clear evidence otherwise; that the denial systems of the parents are usually strong, and most frequently the abuser is uncooperative and will not voluntarily seek help to change his behavior; and that in such cases criminal as well as juvenile court action should be initiated.

Sexual Abuse of Children

176 ROTH, RICHARD. Child Sexual Abuse: Incest, Assault, and
     Sexual Exploitation: A Special Report from the National
     Center on Child Abuse and Neglect. Washington, D.C.:
     Government Printing Office, 1978, 27 pp. Bibliog.
        This concise government report analyzes the scope of
     child sexual abuse and reviews treatment approaches to
     the problem. It offers a tentative definition of child
     sexual abuse and examines incidence figures. It describes
     family dynamics surrounding incest and effects upon children
     and families. The author cites characteristics of success-
     ful treatment and prevention approaches. He concludes with
     a bibliography of approximately seventy-five citations and
     abstracts of fifteen child sexual abuse programs. To order,
     ask the Superintendent of Documents for No. 017-909-00043-7.

177 SPENCER, JOYCE. "Father-Daughter Incest: A Clinical View
     From the Corrections Field." Child Welfare 57, no. 9
     (1978):581-90.
        This overview of father-daughter incest considers, as
     most other studies do, characteristics of each family mem-
     ber and their typical patterns of behavior under the cir-
     cumstances. The article is also concerned with the effect
     of the trial on the child, upon whom the burden and respon-
     sibility of sending the father, usually the breadwinner, to
     jail rests. Since many adolescent girls who experience
     sexual trauma exhibit subsequent self-destructive behavior,
     it is most important to have a well-informed professional
     involved with the victim from the beginning of legal action.
     Like other specialists in this field, Spencer also empha-
     sizes the necessity of having court personnel understand
     the importance of family dynamics in cases of incest.

178 TSAI, MAVIS, and WAGNER, NATHANIEL N. "Incest and Molesta-
     tion: Problems of Childhood Sexuality." Resident and
     Staff Physician 25, no. 3 (March 1979):129-31.
        These researchers present statistics gathered at the
     University of Washington on childhood incest and molesta-
     tion. The two terms are sharply distinguished. Incest
     continues for a long period, from months to years, while
     molestation may be a single incident for the child. The
     key components in any sexual abuse of children are the
     victim's inability to consent to such behavior and the
     likelihood of serious subsequent emotional repercussions.
     The article discusses the extent of the problem, the rela-
     tionship of the offender to the victim, characteristics of
     offenders and victims, effects of the crime, and the role
     of the health professional in assisting victims. The
     stereotype of the child molester who is a total stranger

Treatment Considerations

to the victim is true in fewer than twenty-five percent
of the cases. The authors emphasize the fact that all
children are potential victims of sexual abuse. They conclude that the health professional who is constantly alert
to the possibility of sexual molestation can play a key
role in assisting child victims, as well as adults who are
still harboring psychological wounds from earlier molestation.

179   _____. "Therapy Groups for Women Sexually Assaulted as
       Children." Archives of Sexual Behavior 7, no. 5
       (July 1978):417-27.
           The authors comment upon their therapy groups for women
       who had been sexually assaulted as children. Tsai and
       Wagner feel that the participants' sense of group identi-
       fication helped dispel their feelings of misery, which
       are partly due to the belief that their experiences were
       unique. Also, the primary therapeutic effect was a mitiga-
       tion of guilt and a resultant increase in their self-esteem.
       Their depression and feelings of hopelessness were replaced
       by the mobilizing emotions of anger and a sense of optimism.
       As a result of meeting four times, the participants felt
       able to face the issues immediately. Many became involved
       in other therapeutic processes.

180   WEITZEL, WILLIAM D. et al. "Clinical Management of Father-
       Daughter Incest." American Journal of Diseases of Children
       132, no. 2 (February 1978):127-30.
           Weitzel and his colleagues examine a case in which a
       seventeen-year-old girl was summarily removed from her
       father's home for having had sexual relations with him.
       The community's helping agencies were not engaged in treat-
       ing her or her father. Consequences of their failure to
       act were unfortunate. The authors discuss the case in the
       context of four questions: (1) whether incest per se is
       uniformly harmful to the psychosocial development of the
       child; (2) whether parent and child should be permanently
       separated in all incest cases; (3) whether an exclusive
       focus on the sexual liaison prevents the clinician from
       providing the greatest assistance to the child and family;
       and (4) whether certain therapeutic interventions are more
       effective than others. They advocate a gradual, systematic
       approach as more effective and less wrenching to the girl,
       her father, and to others in her extended family.

181   WESTERMEYER, JOSEPH. "Incest in Psychiatric Practice: A
       Description of Patients and Incestuous Relationships."
       Journal of Clinical Psychiatry 39, no. 8 (August 1978):
       643-48.

Treatment Considerations

This psychiatrist describes the cases of incest he encountered in his practice over a fifteen-year period. He gathered data from thirty-two patients, who included both initiating and receptive partners. Those initiating incest always had lost access to adult sexual partners by death, divorce, illness, or marital partners' disinterest. No one clinical picture predominated. This straightforward, factual account does not indicate the kind of therapy used with the patients.

182   WILLIAMS, GERTRUDE J., and MONEY, JOHN, eds. <u>Traumatic Abuse and Neglect of Children at Home</u>. Baltimore: Johns Hopkins University Press, 1980, 616 pp. Bibliog. and references.
       This book is a collection of papers and studies on many forms of child abuse and neglect. One section, "Responses to Abusive Incest," contains five papers (written between 1954 and 1977) on incest. Four employ psychoanalytic or other psychiatric methods. The Renshaws' study, "Incest" (1977), reviews the subject from biological, psychological, sociological, moral, and legal perspectives. Editor John Money (professor of medical psychology at Johns Hopkins University) introduces the section with a summary of the current professional thinking and a review of the state of the art in treating incestuous families. He mentions the intense moral outrage that obstructs any impartial approach to incest. He feels, however, that sexual abuse undoubtedly results in large measure from parental neglect of their offsprings' early sexual and psychosexual development and education. "In its strictest version the sexual code we live by prescribes avoidance and neglect of sexuality in childhood. . . . In all of the scientific and medical literature, there is not yet a single article on the subject of sexual neglect to counterbalance the articles on sexual abuse."

Chapter 5
Pornography

The impetus to renewed interest in combatting pornography as a portrayal of sexual abuse of women in books, stag magazines, and films may initially have resulted from the Report of President Lyndon Johnson's Commission on Obscenity and Pornography (1970), the result of a two-year investigation costing two million dollars. The Report produced much contention even among the Commission's own members (several of whom wrote minority reports protesting the majority opinion), for the majority statement found no evidence that exposure to or use of explicit sexual materials played a significant role in causing social or individual harm. Nevertheless, it did advocate legislation prohibiting the sale of pornographic materials to young people.

The newly-elected Nixon administration and numerous congress-people totally rejected the report. It is indeed ironic that in 1980 feminists, although viewing the subject from a very different perspective, find substantial agreement with Mr. Nixon's pronouncement in 1970 that a "warped and brutal portrayal of sex . . . if not halted and reversed could poison the wellsprings of American and Western culture and civilization."

Early in the presumed "sexual revolution," young women especially had found it difficult to complain about sexual explicitness for fear of being deemed prudish and repressed. The situation changed, however, with the introduction of "chicken porn" (the displaying of children in titillating sexual acts) and the ever-heightened objectification of women as meat fit for cutting up, stamping, urinating and defecating on, and "snuffing" (murdering), in pornographic films, live performances, and publications. Feminists decided to call a halt to these rawest examples of sadism. Patriarchy's most powerful weapon, resulting in the ultimate degradation of women, had to be stopped.

In November 1978, the first national conference on pornography, "Feminist Perspectives on Pornography," was held in San Francisco. Since that date, several feminist groups on both coasts and in the Midwest have formed a network to coordinate simultaneous "Take Back

the Night" marches, arrange "No More Assaults" months, and conduct
guided tours of districts known for adult bookstores and shops that
specialize in sex tools or toys. These activities have culminated in
all-day seminars to discuss ways and means to combat the multimillion
dollar, crime-connected pornography industry. In addition to the
regular outlets, pornography has appeared in new places, as the high-
fashion industry has jumped aboard the violence bandwagon. Glossy
magazines and storewindow displays indulge in the easy sensationalism
of showing women being beaten up and murdered while modeling glamorous
clothing and makeup. Many people now know of the campaign against
record album jackets and billboard advertising that show women being
brutalized.

Yet effective campaigns against this kind of brutality involve a
difficulty not present in earlier campaigns against rape and battery.
First Amendment freedoms enter the picture. Today feminist lawyers
are grappling with the problem and trying to resolve the dilemma of
how to oppose the brutality in pornography without also censoring
free speech. Censorship is a weapon that could easily be turned
against the Women's Movement by the conservative backlash. The
problem is addressed regularly in Aegis: Magazine on Ending Violence
Against Women, a monthly newsletter published by the National Communi-
cations Network (concerned with battered women), the Feminist Alliance Against Rape, and the Alliance Against Sexual Coercion. In the
September-October 1979 issue of Aegis, lawyer Wendy Kaminer states
the position of Women Against Pornography (a New York City group known
for its strong opposition to pornographic brutality) as one of wanting
to "change the definition of obscenity so that it focuses on violence,
not sex, but we do not propose to alter the basic process by which
obscenity laws must be enforced, in accordance with the procedural
guarantees of the First Amendment. We accept the constitutional limi-
tations on official regulation of speech and we do not expect the
government to magically rid us of pornography." But pornography "is
not a harmless outlet for sexual fantasies. It is fascistic, mi-
sogynist propaganda that fosters acts of violence against women. It
is sexual bondage, not liberation." In the same issue of Aegis,
activist and one-time president of Washington, D.C. NOW, Mary Bailey
writes that civil libertarians must recognize "that society has an
obligation to protect people from the excesses of the rights which
it also protects" and not to allow "a blind willingness to sacrifice
people to abstract principles."

Most of the work that feminists are involved in concerning pornography should allow them to formulate both ideal and practical positions against it. Two basic legal principles must be understood,
namely those of public versus private action, and prior restraint.
These principles are explored in Wendy Kaminer's essay in the May
1980 issue of Newspage, the newsletter of Women Against Violence in
Pornography and the Media WAVPM) in San Francisco. Failure to understand these principles and the one of "clear and present danger"
(which are fairly difficult to grasp and retain) will obstruct an

effective antipornography movement. Kaminer writes: "The feminist movement against pornography must remain an anti-defamation movement, involved in education, consciousness raising, and the development of private strategies against the industry." An important publication in the area, Newspage, can be obtained from WAVPM at P.O. Box 14614, San Francisco, Calif. 94114.

Ms. Magazine and off our backs have crusaded effectively on the subject of pornography and its implications. Ms. reaches many more hundreds of readers than the specialized press could ever hope to do.

A number of studies on the effects of pornography began to appear soon after the publication of the Presidential Commission's Report on Obscenity and Pornography. These studies attempted to measure both psychological and physiological responses to viewing sexually explicit films and photographs. Psychological testing of male and female re-sponses to erotica and pornography continues in various university settings. It forms the basis of reports appearing in a large number of both academic and popular psychological journals. Author Jennifer Fleming (see entry 53) cautions that one should be alert for male bias in the interpretation of experiments that are designed, performed, and evaluated by male psychologists. The following entries list some of these studies. Other entries disclose feminist points of view on how simultaneously to soften the effects of unrestrained free speech while avoiding the trap that censorship lays for the unwary.

CHILD PORNOGRAPHY

183 McKINNON, ISAIAH. "Child Pornography." FBI Law Enforcement
     Bulletin 48, no. 2 (February 1979):18-21.
          This clear, concise article addresses police officers
     investigating child pornography charges. McKinnon, an
     investigator, describes the multimillion dollar business
     and the characteristics of offenders who participate in it.
     He cautions that, no matter how repellent the abuse, offi-
     cers must remember that the child is a victim who probably
     has no real understanding of the crime and that concern,
     patience, and compassion are essential. If McKinnon's
     article is a reliable indicator, it illustrates the adop-
     tion of a more humane technique by the police, similar to
     the approach of other helping professionals.

184 PAYTON, JENNIFER M. "Child Pornography Legislation." Journal
     of Family Law 17, no. 3 (1978-79):505-44.
          Most of what is popularly considered child pornography
     is obscene under present law. Obscenity laws can be en-
     forced through citizen action. There must also be a recon-
     sideration of existing methods of coping with runaway
     children, who have few alternatives for survival besides
     the institutions to which they are sent, where they may be
     subject to sexual abuse as bad, if not worse, as the condi-
     tions from which they have escaped. Shelters must be cre-
     ated without sanctions or strings attached to them. These
     institutions should certainly not be supplying the pornog-
     raphy industry, as many of them now are.

185 POPE, R. S. "Child Pornography: A New Role for the Obscenity
     Doctrine." University of Illinois Law Forum 1978, no. 3:
     711-57.
          By 1978 the federal government and twelve states
     (Arizona, California, Connecticut, Florida, Illinois,
     Louisiana, Minnesota, Missouri, North Dakota, New York,
     Tennessee, and Texas) had enacted legislation against the
     use of children in pornography. Most states structured
     serious criminal penalties around an obscenity standard.
     Previously, the obscenity doctrine had been used to suppress
     offensive sexual films and publications. In this case, it
     protected helpless victims by declaring that child pornog-
     raphers are at least partially accountable for acts of sex-
     ual abuse against children.

186 SCHOETTLE, U. C. "Child Exploitation: A Study of Child
     Pornography." Journal of American Academy of Child
     Psychiatry 19, no. 2 (Spring 1980):289-99.
          Schoettle presents a case study of a twelve-year-old
     girl involved in a child pornography ring. He describes

the similarities and differences between pornography and other forms of sexual abuse. Schoettle identifies three phases in the psychoanalytic treatment of children involved in pornography. In the first phase, the child is engulfed in a flood of emotions--relief that the secret is revealed, but also guilt, anxiety, and further loss of self-esteem. In the second phase, the child's sexual history assumes less importance as her profound anger against parents and members of the ring, especially her sexual intimate (father substitute), takes over. In the third phase, a gradual resumption of normal developmental processes occurs in which the child's sexuality is no longer on graphic display, and she begins to learn nonsexual ways to communicate. The author points out that disclosing prosecution of the adult offender puts the victim in a double bind: if he is acquitted, she feels guilty for not telling enough to insure his punishment; if he is incarcerated, she feels guilty that she is "free." The author also recommends a victim advocate system for children involved in the prosecution of pornography cases.

187   SCHULTZ, LeROY G.   "Kiddie Porn": A Social Policy Analysis. Morgantown: University of West Virginia, 1977, 90 pp. Bibliog.
      This is a full-scale study of the child pornography industry: its origins, producers, consumers, effects, and a review of typical laws against this aspect of child abuse. Schultz's students in the Social Work Graduate School of West Virginia University gathered the data. Schultz states that while most states have child pornography laws under a wide variety of codes, "newly created statutes appear 'symbolic' or 'ceremonial' and are no more enforcible than the older laws dealing with the same problem. They may quiet the public who think something is being done to combat the problem, therefore they are unproductive and misleading."

188   _____. "The Sexual Abuse of Children and Minors: A Bibliography." Child Welfare 58, no. 3 (1979):147-63.
      This is a listing of books and articles without annotations under the following headings: History, Sexual Development, Interviewing Techniques, Sexual Molestation, Incest, Sexual Exploitation, Rape, Treatment and Prevention, The Future, and The Law and Courts.

CULTURAL CONCERNS

189   EISENCK, H. J., and NIAS, D. K. B. <u>Sex, Violence, and the Media</u>. London: Maurice Temple Smith; New York: St. Martin's Press, 1978, 306 pp. Bibliog.

This study examines and rates the relative accuracy of several different methods of investigating the effects of violence and pornography in the media. It is a mistake to say that because researchers often speak tentatively of their findings, "nothing is really known" about the effects of presentations of violence and pornography. All evidence points to the fact that the media's presentation of these subjects affects the viewer. The effects may vary owing to a wide range and combination of personality factors in individuals. But it is clear that in many people sex and aggression are intimately linked and stimulation of one drive can lead to stimulation of the other. The authors insist, controversially, that hormonal factors are more important than socialization in people's development. They strongly criticize sociologists who are unaware of the psychological complexities of the topic or of proper research design and believe that their work is therefore of limited usefulness. The authors believe that censorship is justified when the content of a media presentation is an undeniable incitement to violence and hostile to women.

190   GILMORE, D. H. <u>Sex in Comics: A History of Eight Pagers</u>. 4 vols. San Diego, Calif.: Greenleaf Classics, 1971.

This is a history of approximately 475 pornographic comics published from 1930 to 1965. The majority are from the 1930s and 1940s. They accounted for a multimillion dollar business even in the tight economy of the Great Depression.

191   GOLEMAN, DANIEL, and BUSH, SHERIDA. "The Liberation of Sexual Fantasy." <u>Psychology Today</u> 11, no. 5 (1977):48-53, 104-7.

This article lists all the known "kinky" sex groups in this country today. A de facto coalition of traditional psychoanalysts, religious fundamentalists, and conservatives condemn this kind of sexual activity as perversion or sin. An opposing faction of swingers and therapists promotes sexual experimentation as a nonhurtful, shared experience.

192   JANEWAY, ELIZABETH. <u>Man's World, Woman's Place: A Study in Social Mythology</u>. New York: Delta, 1971, 319 pp. Bibliog.

The first of Janeway's works on the myth of a proper place for women also speaks of the role of pornography as an underpinning for this myth. "It is characteristic of pornography that women submit willingly to outrage and choose victimization. They are raped and fall in love with the rapist, demanding the same treatment again. . . . The purpose of this choice of utter submission is to absolve the man who inflicts the outrages on them of his guilt."

193   MANN, JAY et al. "Evaluating Social Consequences of Erotic Films: An Experimental Approach." Journal of Social Issues 29, no. 3 (1973):113-31.
       The authors detail yet another experiment that attempts to measure subjects' aggressive behavior as a result of viewing pornographic films.

194   PALMER, C. E. "Pornographic Comics: A Content Analysis." Journal of Sex Research 15, no. 4 (November 1979):285-98.
       This research documents, through content analyses, the nature of pornographic themes in a collection of pornographic comics usually called 'eight-pagers.' Females and males exhibit similar carnal appetite and sexual aggression. Many comics display chauvinism and male fantasies. Comics project 'normative' sexuality by concentrating upon adult monogamous heterosexual behavior. The author discusses taxonomical, linguistic, and methodological problems in studying pornographic comics. Future studies of sex comics may answer the basic questions of whether pornocomics could possibly serve as therapeutic tools for those with particular sexual problems; could express and mold commonly held values; could offer a means of studying deviant behavior; and could aid in understanding cultural differences. The answers to these questions may make us more sensitive to various subtleties of other forms of social and sexual behavior.

195   PRESIDENT'S COMMISSION ON OBSCENITY AND PORNOGRAPHY. Report. Washington, D.C.: Government Printing Office, 1970, 646 pp.
       A commission of eighteen members appointed by President Lyndon Johnson in 1968 conducted a massive study of the pornography industry in this country. Over a two-year period, the commission's several subcommittees attempted to assess the effects of a number of pornographic wares (such as films, books, magazines, and sexual devices) of service establishments, and of the inroads made by organized crime into the pornography industry on the quality of

Cultural Concerns

life in this country. Dissension among the commission members developed almost immediately and resulted in both
majority and minority reports to the President and to
Congress. The majority report recommended relaxing legal
restraints on the production of pornography and penalizing
those involved in this business. Repression ultimately
would serve little purpose. Of the eighteen members of
the commission only two were women, especially notable
since pornography ultimately has a more violent impact
upon women than upon men.

196 ROSENFIELD, LAWRENCE W. "Politics and Pornography." Quarterly
Journal of Speech 59, no. 4 (December 1973):413-22.
This article suggests that pornography functions as a
surrogate for freedom and the popularity of a particular
theme in sexual literature is symptomatic of the frustration of an associated politico-socio-psychological need.
There are references to personal observations, literary
criticism, and sociological surveys, as well as speculation
on motives. Rosenfield asserts that (a) purchasers of
pornographic materials feel imprisoned by their daily,
respectable surroundings; (b) spokespersons for conven-
tional piety oppose distribution of pornography as a violent public act; and (c) decaying civilizations increase
their output of decadent literature as opportunities for
self-fulfillment contract.

197 SARRIS, ANDREW. Politics and Cinema. New York: Columbia
University Press, 1978, 215 pp.
In the chapter "The Politics of Pornography," Sarris, a
respected film critic, compares pornographic movies he has
viewed. His opinions will be argued or appreciated by
those filmgoers who never miss a showing; however, Sarris
appears to think little of most of the films: "Many critics
have been waging a devious campaign to make hard-core pornography seem more 'truthful' and more 'authentic' than
soft-core or simulated pornography."

198 SOBEL, LESTER A., ed. Pornography, Obscenity and the Law.
New York: Facts on File, 1979, 187 pp.
This is a clear, concise exposition of the history of
the treatment of pornography and obscenity in America. It
includes discussion of the legal background and early concern with obscenity: the role of organized crime in the
production and distribution of pornographic materials; the
Pornography Commission's Report; ways in which pornography

is dealt with in motion pictures, live theater, broadcast-
ing, and in the mail; child pornography; and significant
court decisions.

FEMINIST RESPONSE

199   Aegis: Magazine on Ending Violence Against Women. Washington,
       D.C.: National Communication Network, the Feminist Alli-
       ance Against Rape, and the Alliance Against Sexual Coercion.
          Aegis is published six times yearly by the above organi-
       zations, composed of activists working to end violence
       against women. Its statement of purpose announces: "To
       this end, Aegis provides practical information and resources
       for grassroots organizers, along with promoting a continuing
       discussion among feminists of the root causes of rape, bat-
       tering, sexual harassment and other forms of violence
       against women." For subscriptions, address: FAAR, P. O.
       Box 21033, Washington, D.C. 20009.

200   BARRY, KATHLEEN. Female Sexual Slavery. Englewood Cliffs,
       N.J.: Prentice-Hall, 1979, 274 pp.
          Kathleen Barry joins Susan Brownmiller (Against Our Will),
       Mary Daly (GYN/ECOLOGY), and Susan Griffin (Rape and the
       Power of Consciousness) in extracting from the contemporary
       and historical morass of political and social reality the
       horrifying structure of the enslavement of women. She
       catalogs brutish treatment in accepted cultural modes and
       reveals the pattern of total power wielded by patriarchal
       systems worldwide in controlling women. Barry contributes
       three significant elements to the growing literature on
       misogyny. (1) She exposes the fact that an International
       Criminal Police Organization (INTERPOL) report, "Traffic in
       Women: Recent Trends," prepared for the United Nations
       Division of Human Rights, was kept off the agenda of the
       International Women's Year Conference in Mexico City in
       1975 because the UN has a vested interest in hiding female
       slavery. (2) She coins the term "sex colonization" to
       describe men's private control of women within the social
       and political order. "Institutionalized sexism and misog-
       yny--from discrimination in employment to dehumanization in
       pornography--stem from the primary sexual domination of
       women in one to one situations. . . ." (3) In her chapter
       on Patricia Hearst, whom Barry sees as the paradigm of a
       female slave, she maintains that, hated and reviled by
       both her captors and the world at large after she had

Feminist Response

assumed the persona of Tania, Hearst may be regarded as a
representative of all women forced into slavery, who, in
order to continue to exist at all, must accept the only
path allowed them. Hearst's personal strength changed her
from being a victim to being a survivor.

201   CARTER, ANGELA. The Sadeian Woman and the Ideology of Pornog-
      raphy. New York: Pantheon, 1979, 154 pp. Bibliog.
          A polemical preface explains the philosophy of pornog-
      raphy, which functions solely to annihilate women. Carter
      describes how de Sade stands at the threshhold of the modern
      period when the substance of human nature and social institu-
      tions was debated as freely as in our own time. His writing
      concerns the nature of sexual freedom. Of particular sig-
      nificance to women is his refusal to see female sexuality
      in relation to its reproductive function. Today the func-
      tion of women as primarily reproductive beings is questioned.
      In her description and explication of Sadeian heroines,
      Carter compares our modern versions of these heroines--May
      West, Mary Pickford, Marilyn Monroe--to Justine and Juliette,
      powerless females in a patriarchal, libertine world. "It
      is fair to say that when pornography serves--as with very
      rare exceptions it always does--to reinforce the prevailing
      system of values and ideas in a given society, it is toler-
      ated; and when it does not, it is banned."

202   FRIEDMAN, DEB. "Feminist Perspective on Pornography." off
      our backs 9, no. 1 (January 1979):2-3.
          Friedman reports on the first feminist conference on
      pornography held in San Francisco, November 1978.

203   KELLY, JANIS, and MOIRA, FRAN. "A Clear and Present Danger."
      off our backs 9, no. 1 (January 1979):7.
          The article explains why pornography should be more, not
      less, visible.

204   McCORMACK, THELMA. "Machismo in Media Research: A Critical
      Review of Research on Violence and Pornography." Social
      Problems 25, no. 5 (June 1978):544-55.
          McCormack examines two areas of media research in an
      attempt to account for the discrepancy in their findings
      on pornography and violence. Pornography is considered to
      be innocuous, while violent scenes are serious and warrant
      censorship. McCormack claims that both sets of research
      have sexist biases in the way problems are conceptualized
      and in their research designs. She suggests that the

underlying reason for the discrepancy is a machismo orientation defined as a narcissistic pride in sexual virility
(pornography), the other side of which is anxiety about
male sexual identity. Also, the instruments used by the
investigators perpetuate the myth of female sexual passivity. She proposes ways in which some sociological theory
(reference group theory and F-scale research) can eliminate
bias.

205   MORGAN, ROBIN. "How to Run the Pornographers Out of Town (and
      Preserve the First Amendment)." Ms. 7, no. 5
      (November 1978):55
         Robin Morgan faces the issue of pornography squarely.
      She notes that the President's Commission of Obscenity and
      Pornography (1970) suppressed some of the causal links be-
      tween pornography, on the one hand, and rape and brutality
      toward women, on the other. She suggests several possible
      reasons: the pornography industry wields political power;
      only two of the eighteen commissioners were women; research-
      ers are not immune from cultural biases. Morgan urges women
      to demand their right to move freely without fear of the
      psychological degradation and physical danger that pornog-
      raphy inspires and sanctions. She sees an escalation in
      misogyny, with rape, mutilation, and murder viewed as aver-
      age sexual acts, and with a "normal" man depicted as a sad-
      ist and a "healthy" woman as willing victim. The difference
      between soft-core and hard-core categories of pornography
      has blurred: Indicators are the "brutality chic" of the
      high-fashion magazines, department storewindows, "snuff"
      films and rock album jackets, and child pornography movies
      that now play in first-run movie theaters. In fact, the
      Wall Street Journal has described the industry as a major
      business linked with organized crime, sex kidnappings, and
      sexual libertarian publicity campaigns. Morgan's widely-
      quoted phrase--"Pornography is the theory; rape and molesta-
      tion the practice"--expresses her summary of the situation.
      She states that it is possible to be opposed to pornography
      and in favor of the First Amendment. Morgan suggests that
      we must investigate the Constitutional protections inherent
      in such principles as prohibitions on interfering with the
      civil rights of others and inciting to violence.

206   Newspage. San Francisco, Calif.: Women Against Violence in
      Pornography and Media.
         This monthly newsletter explores the many destructive
      aspects of pornography and informs readers of efforts by
      feminist groups to counteract its effects. For membership
      and subscriptions: P.O. Box 14614, San Francisco, Calif.:
      94114.

Feminist Response

207   STEINEM, GLORIA. "Erotica and Pornography: A Clear and Present Difference." <u>Ms</u>. 7, no. 5 (November 1978):53-54.
      Steinem speaks of pornography and erotica as being crucially different, in fact, although confused in many people's minds. Both assume that sexuality should be separated from reproduction and used to convey a personal message. The conservative religious backlash, however, condemns all sexuality not linked to marriage and childbirth, out of a fear of women's progress toward independence. It is assumed the whole patriarchal structure would collapse as a result. The reactionary groups therefore denounce printed materials about abortion and women's control over their bodies and attempt to invoke the obscenity law against the mailing of such materials. The liberal or radical "intellectual" male counterpart to religious conservatives exacts vengeance against the Women's Movement by defending pornography and appealing to the freedom guaranteed by the First Amendment. In either case, sex reinforces inequality. Females must either accept their "destiny" and devote themselves to bearing and rearing young or accept the domination of men through brutality. One alternative to work toward is making competent, rather than childlike women, symbols of the erotic, or loving, message.

PSYCHOLOGICAL EFFECTS

208   BERKOWITZ, LEONARD. "Sex and Violence: We Can't Have It Both Ways." <u>Psychology Today</u> 5, no. 7 (December 1971): 14, 18-23.
      The President's Commissions on the Causes and Prevention of Violence and on Obscenity and Pornography essentially concluded that exposure to media presentation of violence or pornography yields temporary stimulation. The former Commission suggested limiting media violence; the latter Commission suggested relaxing restrictions on pornography. Recommendations were influenced by unidentified variables. Only a small portion of an audience may be influenced toward violence or deviant sexual behavior. The probability of encouraging such behavior cannot be ignored. In fact, the risk should be rationally considered.

209   DONNERSTEIN, EDWARD, and HALLAN, JOHN. "Facilitating Effects of Erotica on Aggression Against Women." <u>Journal of Personality and Social Psychology</u> 36 (September 1978):1270-77.

Pornography

Psychological Effects

     This article reports on a series of psychological experi-
mentations designed to examine increasing male attacks
against women caused by viewing several erotic and aggressive films.

210   FESHBACH, S., AND MALAMUTH, N. "Sex and Aggression: Proving
      Link." Psychology Today (12 November 1978):111-18, 122.
      Feshbach and Malamuth of the University of California at
      Los Angeles (UCLA) were among the first experimental psy-
      chologists to identify the close link between sex and vio-
      lence in our society. A series of experiments with many
      different variables suggested that men who regularly view
      portrayals of aggressive sex in books, magazines, and films
      are more stimulated by the idea of rape and less sympathetic
      to victims. This conclusion differs from those of the
      President's Commission on Obscenity and Pornography. A
      typical UCLA experiment allowed subjects to view an erotic
      film or read an erotic passage and then provided them with
      opportunities to act aggressively against a colleague of
      the experimenter. A series of preset errors by the col-
      league (who was given a simulated electric shock by the
      subject) provided the experimenter with an index of the
      subjects' levels of agression. Feshback maintained, how-
      ever, that arousal models failed to account for the special
      meaning of sex and aggression in our culture. Further ex-
      perimentation suggested that aggression is subdued when
      sexual arousal was accompanied by inhibitory feelings. He
      proposed, therefore, that sexual arousal alone does not
      stimulate aggression. If accompanied by a reduction in
      sexual inhibition, it will generalize into aggressive be-
      havior, especially where common taboos affect sex and
      aggression. These experimenters believe that psychologists
      ought not to support, explicitly or implicitly, the use of
      pornography to reduce aggressive tendencies in male patients,
      for in pornography violence is the theme; it is never a
      part of a larger drama. Pornography even approximates a
      how-to-do-it manual. It carries the message that inflict-
      ing pain and humiliation on a victim can be fun and en-
      courages the relaxation of inhibitions against rape.

211   GIBBONS, FREDERICK. "Sexual Standards and Reactions to
      Pornography." Journal of Personality and Social Psychology
      36 (September 1978):976-87.
      The article investigates the impact of society's sexual
      standards upon reactions to pornography.

212   LEVITT, E. E. "Some New Perspectives on an Old Problem." The
      Journal of Sex Research 5, no. 4 (November 1969):247-59.

97

Psychological Effects

> This article appeared in 1969, before the Women's Move-
> ment had begun trying to make the public sensitive to the
> fact that pornography is a cause of violence toward women.
> Levitt asserts that no form of visual erotica is in itself
> guilty or innocent of any charge one may bring against it.
> Only well-designed and well-executed research carried out
> by impartial social scientists [undoubtedly male, Ed.]
> uncommitted to any sectarian hypothesis could possibly
> answer the question. He maintains further that a rela-
> tively inoffensive stimulus may be more arousing than
> blatantly sexual stimuli. His tabulation of erotica by
> class (obscenity, smut, pornography); by level of language
> (presence or absence of "hard-core" words, scatology); and
> by whether or not graphic portrayals of suggestive sexual
> acts were static or in motion attempted to show that all
> human experience is a series of exclusively sexual events.

213   STOLLER, ROBERT J. "Pornography and Perversion." Archives of
      General Psychiatry 22, no. 6 (1970):490-99.
      Pornography exposes the dynamics of such perversions as
      voyeurism, sadism, and masochism. Each user seeks out the
      type of behavior most relevant to him, that is, a sadist
      seeks depictions of sadistic acts and a transvestite, acts
      of cross-dressing. The unconscious memory of past life
      history events is expressed consciously in particular por-
      nographic materials. Pornography varies according to life
      history and psychodynamics. All forms illustrate the sur-
      mounting of danger (experienced as humiliation, anxiety,
      fear, or frustration). All pornography contains the psy-
      chodynamics of perversion. For the most part, it is aimed
      at heterosexual men. It serves to resolve conflict, dis-
      tress, frustration, and anger. Stoller also treat women's
      reactions to pornography.

Chapter 6
Conclusion: The Government Reacts

In concluding this bibliography, it will probably be helpful for readers to know the contributions of the federal government, Congress, and state and local governments toward solving the pervasive problem of violence against women in all its many aspects. The Equal Rights Amendment (ERA) is by far the most important symbol of renewal in women's lives. It would signal the beginning of more dramatic and far-reaching improvements where mere tokens exist today. Yet as of July 1980, its eventual passage is uncertain. Resistance to passage remains stubborn, perhaps increasing in some quarters.

Short of passage of the ERA, here are some of the ways the federal government is responding to women's pressure on a number of fronts, especially regarding domestic violence. In April 1979, the Carter Administration created the Interdepartmental Committee on Domestic Violence. The Department of Health and Human Services (HHS) established an Office on Violence that administers a clearinghouse on domestic violence, coordinates related HHS programs, and supports public education and research and demonstration programs in the field.

Other federal agencies have allocated varying amounts of funding for a range of programs. For example, the Law Enforcement Assistance Administration (LEAA) had funded some twenty-five service or demonstration projects by the close of 1979. The Department of Housing and Urban Development (HUD) has provided some funds for local shelters for battered women through its Women's Policy and Programs division. The National Center on Child Abuse and Neglect, within HHS, has given grants to investigate child sexual abuse, among other problems. The National Institute for Alcohol Abuse and Alcoholism assists projects dealing with alcohol-related domestic violence. Some funds from Title XX of the Social Security Act have been channeled into shelters. Other support comes from the ACTION-funded National Technical Assistance Center on Family Violence, the National Legal Resource Center for Child Advocacy and Protection, and the National Victim/Witness Resource Center.

The United States House of Representatives passed legislation known as the Domestic Violence Prevention and Services Act in

December 1979. A related measure expected in 1980, however, failed to receive legislative approval in November.

Agencies at lower levels of government have invested resources in countering violence against women. Cities and counties appear to be less reluctant to assist grassroots groups. State justice departments are instituting family violence units. Special training for police is on the increase. The criminal justice system is beginning to support victim/witness advocates. Especially where state coalitions against domestic violence or sexual assault are strong, there is state legislative activity acknowledging public responsibility.

Extensive creative effort and energy have been devoted to designing programs to reduce violence against women and produce high levels of public awareness and understanding. Nevertheless, feminists have to admit that the censorship activities of political conservatives and religious fundamentalists, often one and the same, quite seriously hamper efforts to make much excellent information available. Proof of the far Right's successful campaigns surfaces in numerous communities where important basic information, such as the book Our Bodies, Ourselves, has been removed from public schools and public libraries. The far Right insists, moreover, that progressive legislative programs and criminal justice training programs, for example, not only waste taxpayers' money but also threaten the values of traditional Christian nuclear families. Sustaining the momentum to make the public aware and public policy responsive largely depends upon successfully resisting the activities of the conservative backlash.

Author/Title Index

References are to entry numbers, not pages.

Notman, Malkah T., 123

Obscenity and Pornography,
    President's Commission Report
    on, 195
On Lies, Secrets, and Silence,
    Selected Prose 1966-1978, 16
"On Writing a History of Rape,"
    152
O'Sullivan, Elizabeth Ann, 142
"Overview of Legal Remedies for
    Battered Women," 52
Owens, D. M., 37

Paddock, John, 15
Palmer, C. E., 194
Patriarchal Attitudes: The Case
    for Women in Revolt, 9
Payne, Elaine Johnson, 141
Payton, Jennifer M., 184
"Penalties for Rape as a Function
    of Victim Provocativeness,"
    111
"Personal and Social Psycho-
    pathology and the Primary
    Prevention of Violence," 27
Pethick, Jane, 47
Pizzey, Erin, 66
"Police Attitudes Toward Rape
    Before and After a Training
    Program," 107
Politics and Cinema, 197
"Politics and Pornography," 196
Politics of the Family and Other
    Essays, The, 13
Politics of Rape, The: The
    Victim's Perspective, 143
Pope, R. S., 185
"Pornographic Comics: A Content
    Analysis," 194
"Pornography and Perversion,"
    213
Pornography, Obscenity and the
    Law, 198
"Power, Sex, and Violence: The
    Case of Marital Rape," 137
"Predicting Rape Victim
    Reportage," 138
President's Commission on Obscen-
    ity and Pornography, 195
Price, John, 67

"Protecting Personal Space:
    Victim and Resister Reactions
    to Assaultive Rape," 126
"Psychodynamics of Violence-Prone
    Marriages, The," 74
"Psychological, Cultural and
    Family Factors in Incest and
    Family Sexual Abuse," 157
"Psychological Significance of
    Rape: Some Aspects," 127
"Psychosocial Aspects of Wife
    Battering," 72

Rader, Charles M., 124
Rape: A Bibliography, 100
"Rape: A Review Essay," 146
"Rape: A Sexual Deviation," 119
"Rape and Physical Attractiveness:
    Assigning Responsibility to
    Victim," 125
Rape and Rape-related Issues:
    An Annotated Bibliography,
    102
"Rape as a Social Problem: A
    By-Product of the Feminist
    Movement," 109
Rape Bibliography, The: A Col-
    lection of Abstracts, 103
Rape: Crisis and Recovery, 116
"Rape: Disclosure to Parental
    Family Members," 117
"Rape Law Reform and Women's
    Equality," 110
"Rape Myths: In Legal, Theoret-
    ical and Everyday Practice,"
    144
"Rape: Power, Anger, and Sex-
    uality," 120
"Rape: The All-American Crime,"
    148
Rape: The First Sourcebook for
    Women, 135
"Rape: The Husband's and Boy-
    friend's Initial Reactions,"
    139
Rape: The Power of Consciousness,
    149
Rape: The Price of Coercive
    Sexuality, 104
"Rape Victim, The: Psychodynamic
    Considerations," 123

Subject Index

History of women, general
survey, 7
Housewives, 3
Humanistic psychology, 111, 174

Incest, 116; acting out of ado-
lescent girls, 177; American
Psychiatric Association report on, 156; attitudes of
judicial system, 166, 169,
170, 177; attitudes of medical personnel, 166; attitudes of police, 177;
clinical types of 164, 181;
community services, 165, 166,
173, 175; family characteristics in, 157, 162, 166,
167, 170, 172, 173, 174,
175, 176, 177, 178, 180;
genetic aspects of, 155,
169; guidelines for determining, 159, 163, 165, 178;
interagency cooperation in
treatment of, 175; laws
against, 169; legal aspects
of, 155, 159, 162, 169, 174;
origins of, 155, 161; personal accounts, 153, 154;
psychological aspects, 121,
154, 155, 157, 161, 166,
168, 169, 172, 176, 178,
179, 180; recommendations to
end abuse, 172, 172, 176;
reported positive aspects of,
156; research, 158, 161, 182,
176; SIECUS report on, 156;
supportive services for victims, 167, 171; treatment
models, 162, 165, 168, 170,
172, 173, 174, 176, 180;
trends toward decriminaliza-
tion, 156. See also Child
pornography, sexual victimization of children
Intergenerational communication,
13

Judaic tradition, 9
Just-world theory, 30, 105

Legitimization of violence, 29,
31, 32, 35, 201

Marital rape, 38, 137, 143
Masochism, 9, 28, 71, 73
Medical personnel, attitudes, 61,
62
Mikulski-Muller Domestic Violence
Bill (HR 2977), 58
Minnesota Multiphasic Personality
Inventory (MMPI), 124
Misogyny, 16, 33, 149, 201

National Center on Child Abuse
and Neglect, 177
National Coalition Against
Domestic Violence, 53
National Commission on the
Observance of International
Women's Year, 19
National Criminal Justice Refer-
ence Service, 45
National Plan of Action (1977),
19

Objectification of women, 31,
201

Patriarchy, 8, 9, 11, 16, 17, 27,
31, 32, 33, 147, 148, 149,
151
Police, attitudes, 51. See also
Battered women, attitudes of
police; Incest, attitudes of
police; Rape, attitudes of
police
Pornographic comics, 190, 194
Pornography and conservative
opposition, 207; and degradation of women, 205; and
erotica, 207, 209; and First
Amendment, 203, 205, 207;
and libertarian perspective,
207; and myth of women's
place, 192; and sexual experimentation, 191; and violence against women, 209,
210; as political expression,
196; censorship of, 189;